SOUL SOURCE

A SOUL SERIES VOLUME

ROSIE CHEE

ISBN 979-8-89243-519-2 (paperback)
ISBN 979-8-89243-520-8 (digital)

Copyright © 2025 by Rosie Chee

All rights reserved. No part of this publication may be reproduced, distributed, or transmitted in any form or by any means, including photocopying, recording, or other electronic or mechanical methods without the prior written permission of the publisher. For permission requests, solicit the publisher via the address below.

Christian Faith Publishing
832 Park Avenue
Meadville, PA 16335
www.christianfaithpublishing.com

Printed in the United States of America

THE SOUL SERIES

SOUL SOURCE
SOUL STORM
SOUL SURF

Though loosely labeled volumes (SOURCE, STORM, SURF), consecutive "carry on" from the previous, "telling a story" in its own way, each volume in the Soul Series a standalone work (and every piece can be read in or out of order).

SOUL ARTIST

A different kind of work undefined by any single "term", taking creative liberty in freesoul expression of truth and consciousness as experienced in emotions and feelings that inspire and illuminate the passion and purpose of existence.

SOUL SOURCE

SOUL

SOUL is energy. It is who we are. Our core essence. Our truth. We are all stories. Our souls go through seasons. Every chapter is both beginning and ending.

SOURCE

Souls are each a universe contained in skin, orphic and unique unto and in of itself. Life leaves none untouched, experiences affecting every soul differently. Ultimately, everything we live serves to teach and allow for constant becoming more of what we are: Truth of the SOURCE that whispers and speaks.

SPREAD LIGHT

You can BE the light in the world or you can be the mirror REFLECTING the light of change that you want to see. Are you a leader or a follower? Determining what you are will influence whether you are the light or the reflection.

BE the change you want to see. BE the light you want to see illuminated in the lives of the people you touch. BE the difference you want to make. BE the example you want others to follow. BE the one that CREATES the change, the one looked up to, the one who inspires POSITIVE effect.

If you do not have it within you to be the one that stands up and out, but you want your life to make a difference, to illuminate the light that is in your heart, be a MIRROR and reflect it out into the world, spreading the light of hope and faith that way.

You are stronger than you THINK. You have MORE within you than you believe. You CAN be the light if you desire to be. It's YOUR choice. Either way, SPREAD the light of life and hope and faith and change out in the world and MAKE a difference. Always remember, I DECIDE!

> "Every single person on the planet has a story. Don't judge people before you truly know them. The truth might surprise you."

> "Never compare your journey with others. Your path is unique. Own it and make the best out of it."

[α]

WE ARE ALL HERE TO HELP EACH OTHER. MAKE A DIFFERENCE FOR THE BETTER. ENCOURAGE OTHER SOULS TO HEIGHTS THEY MAY NEVER HAVE IMAGINED. ACCEPTING UNCONDITIONALLY AND WITHOUT JUDGEMENT. A "SAFE SPACE" TO ALLOW OTHERS TO SIMPLY JUST "BE".

[α] Photographer: Tony Mitchell.

BENEATH THE SURFACE

That face. Those words. These actions. There is an entirely DIFFERENT world going on behind these eyes looking out at the rest of this world. A world most will never see or know of because they concern themselves with only what APPEARS to be and never bother to look BENEATH the surface to what IS.

Never let what you SEE dictate what you KNOW. There is a soul behind those eyes that you can now see glimmer through that stayed hidden for so long. There is a heart mashed in there somewhere deep down that wants to have no fear but hesitates sometimes because it remembers what hurt is like as if it were not a memory, even though it knows the people in the now are NOT those of the past. There is constant pain of body, pushed through DAILY, sometimes an accomplishment all itself, just being able to move and appear "normal" and "okay".

Everyone has something you will likely NEVER know of, so before you assume or judge, ASK. You might be surprised by what you discover. You might be surprised by the person you find. Life is a miracle and we are ALL miracles in it. VALUE it and always seek the seed of a soul, not the bud that appears to close itself to the world.

EVERYONE HAS A STORY

You have a story. I have a story. EVERYone has a story. A story about life, an event, a period, a moment, a truth; something significant that changed, whether it be in an instant or over time. Everyone has a beginning, middle, and end; some are just starting, whilst others are nearing the finish line.

What you see is NOT reality; it is not what WAS or what CAN be or what WILL be. It simply is what is right NOW, and "right now" can change in an instant. You canNOT look at a person and know what they have been through, where they have come from; you canNOT assume that just because someone LOOKS fit and healthy that they have ALWAYS been fit and healthy, or even that they ARE fit and healthy; what one LOOKS like is no indicator of what they truly are INSIDE. Sure, looks may help reflect the lifestyle a person leads, even in fitness, but it does not mean that they ARE as they appear.

So before you are quick to have an IMPRESSION of someone you know NOTHING about, take the time to GET to know them. Ask them who they are and where they have been; more importantly, WHERE they are going and what they are taking from their experience. Where one has been gives you an understanding of where they are at now, and can help motivate not just them, but YOU as well, FORWARD.

You might be surprised to learn that the trainer who looks like a fitness model was once the "fat kid" at school, tormented until they reached a breaking point and turned their life around. Or that the woman who trains like someone possessed lives in constant physical pain every day, pushing through the pain because she knows the end result is worth enduring more pain.

Or that the most motivating person you know projects positivity to hide the pain they feel inside, knowing that if they cannot help themselves at least they can inspire others to do great things.

What would you do if you KNEW these things? Would it change your PERSPECTIVE? Would it improve your AWARENESS? Would it make a DIFFERENCE?

EVERYONE has a story and you never know unless you ASK or they SHARE. You never know the impact YOUR story could have on another's life, the difference knowing what you have been through and struggle with could have on someone you do not even know. So do not be afraid to let others know where you have been and what you have overcome to be where you are today.

It's about COMMUNITY, making a DIFFERENCE, being there to HELP others create a BETTER life. SHARE TO INSPIRE!

BE WHO YOU WERE MEANT TO BE

Every experience we have becomes part of who we are, but how we choose to let those experiences affect us is our choice. The past is gone. Learn from it and move on. Although it may have helped shape us into the person that we are today, we are not what we were then and never will be again.

There is no point in living in a day already long gone, so quit putting yourself in a little box by trying to live consistently with your past and explaining every little action you take. Be you. Fully! In this moment. Independent of what others may or may not expect from you.

If you're not who you want to be, do something about it! Change. Become who you want to be and don't let anyone try and make you into something else! Your life is your own. Live it how you want to!

WHO WILL YOU BECOME?

Decide WHO you want to be. Make sure it's someone you can be PROUD of. Be someone who leads by EXAMPLE. Make a life that creates DIFFERENCE in the lives you touch.

WHAT WILL YOU CHOOSE TO BE?

ROSIE "FEMALE TERMINATOR" CHEE

β

β Photographer: Tony Mitchell.

CHOOSE TO BE A WARRIOR!

We are what we CHOOSE to become! Through the trials and triumphs of life, we are moulded into something more than could ever have been imagined when we were born. When we fall, whether we allow ourselves to keep falling and hit the ground, or whether we try and spread our wings to fly; if we hit the ground, whether we are beaten and stay down or stand and strive to take ourselves back to the heights we fell from. When we love and lose that love, whether we allow the pain to strengthen or destroy us; if it destroys us, whether we will lock our heart away forever or find the courage to risk everything again. When we face death, whether we accept it or stand and fight; if we fight, whether it changes us and gives us a new appreciation for and perspective on life. All these things, amongst MANY others, mould and create us, temper our soul into the defeated or a WARRIOR.

Choose to LIVE life with PASSION and DETERMINATION! Choose to NEVER give up! Choose to be everything you were MEANT to be! Choose to be a WARRIOR!

DREAM LIFE

Have a dream but never had the courage to go after it? PURSUE it! Have a hope that you thought would always be a hope and nothing more? ACT on it! Have a thought that has lain deep inside your soul waiting for the right moment to be revealed? SHARE it! Have another side of you that you have never dared show the world? Let it OUT! Have something you have wanted more than anything but are not sure if the reality is going to be as much as the fantasy of it? DECIDE today! MAKE LIFE HAPPEN!

If you want to change your life, CHANGE it! It all starts with YOU! YOU make the decisions, the choices, create the actions, the ripples of effect that spread out as a result of your desire and passions. If life is not going the way you want it to, not as full and complete as it should be, not as inspired as you know it has potential, then take a stand and turn around TO make it as it SHOULD be! It's NEVER too late to change and every dawn is the chance to start OVER, to make it what you WANT!

ARE YOU A DREAMER OR A VISIONARY?

A dreamer dreams, but that is all they do. They are content to simply dream and never act, afraid that if they pursue such dreams they might lose what they already have, that things will change, but mostly because they either do not believe in themselves or they fear failure.

On the other hand, a visionary dreams, but they also act and do all they can to turn those dreams into reality. They have a vision of the future and they are not content to just dream about it. They set goals and plan a journey towards the realization of their dreams, knowing that a dream is only the beginning of things, willing to take the risk and follow that dream wherever it may lead them.

It's good to have dreams. It's even better to have dreams and pursue them!

MAKE LIFE HAPPEN!

Life doesn't go slow and if you're not careful, time will pass you by before you even know it. Therefore make the most of every day, take every chance and opportunity you are given, try and make a difference, risk whatever you are willing to make your life an experience you will never forget!

Not every opportunity we want we are going to be given in life, and sometimes if we want something, we have to create that opportunity ourselves! Those who know what they want take the risk and go after it, making it happen! Nothing happens by sitting still and hoping that it happens to you; you've got to make it happen! If you don't take the risk, you'll never know what could have been.

Make the most of your present, to create the best future for yourself! To get the greatest rewards, you have to take the greatest risks. Life is not about playing it safe and hoping that something good will happen! It's about MAKING that something happen!

NOTHING IS IMPOSSIBLE!

What would you dare to accomplish if you knew that the only possible outcome was success? What would you dare to do if you knew that you could not fail? What is your ultimate dream and what is holding you back from daring all to achieve it?

There is nothing wrong with reaching for the stars; in fact, I encourage it! Impossible is nothing. There is almost always a way. So why not dream the ultimate dream? Why not set yourself the task of starting on the journey to accomplish that dream?

It may take days, weeks, months, or even years to achieve that ultimate dream, but better to achieve it than to simply sit by and let time pass you by as you wish you could. After all, life is in the LIVING, in the journey to that dream, in learning along the way, bettering yourself as you grow closer and closer to your destination.

IT'S TIME

It's time to stop JUST dreaming and start DOING. It's time to start ACTING on the secret desires hidden in your heart. It's time to begin living the life you WANT to have. It's time to CREATE the you in your soul for the world to SEE.

It's time to STOP letting OTHERS dictate your life. It's time to start taking CONTROL of your own destiny. It's time to begin accepting ALL responsibility for the consequences that happen in your life. It's time to create the FUTURE you WANT.

It's time to stop looking and COMPARING yourself to OTHERS. It's time to start realizing that it is YOUR actions determining the path your life takes. It's time to begin ascending the mountain that will take you to the STARS. It's time to create YOUR masterpiece.

No one is holding you back but YOU. When you assume that ACCOUNTABILITY you can start making things happen FOR you. You can begin to see what has to be done and HOW. You ENABLE yourself to create a dream in reality. IT'S TIME.

WHAT IS "NORMAL"?

What is "normal"? Is there a "normal"? If you want my honest opinion, I don't think there is. If there is, to be "normal" is to follow the crowd and be what others expect you to be, instead of following your heart and soul and being the person that you were meant to be. In that case, you are allowing yourself to simply be, to "settle" in life, never to step out of your comfort zone and take risks, content to forever stay the same, never rising above the crowd, blending in so that no one knows you from the person next to you.

If that's "normal", then why be "normal"? What's the appeal? Don't you want to stand out and be different? Don't you want to think for yourself and have your own ideals? Don't you want to be in charge of your own destiny and set the wheels in motion for achieving those things "normal" people think are impossible? Wouldn't you rather be a doer than a follower, a pioneer, someone others look up to, a positive role model to the masses of "normal"?

Everyone is unique. There is no one person like you in the entire world, who is, has been, or ever will be. You were not created "normal" and you are not intended to be "normal". So stand out, be different, walk your own path, and just be you!

LISTEN

Listen to your soul. Feel your heart. Act on your intuition. Believe there's a reason. Where are you led? What or who calls? Why does it persist? There's always a reason.

Sometimes you just have to take the chance. You have to take the risk. You have to take that first step. You have to find out why you are drawn so to wherever or whatever or whomever.

You have to know that your soul does not long for something without purpose. Your heart and mind might be able to lie, but your soul cannot. Your soul always speaks truth. You just have to pay attention and know when to listen.

KEEP THE FIRE BURNING

We all start somewhere, no matter who we are. Some of us start earlier down the road than others, and some are well along the stages of their journey when they head off down another path that will become another mission. No matter who you are or where you have been, you can always start over, have before you that fresh slate, ready to write a new history for yourself.

We all have our own reasons for getting started, for wanting to achieve something, for pursuing a dream. We all have the initial desire and motivation that propels us into action. Sometimes though, it's hard to keep that passion burning as brightly as it did when we first started out. When that happens, we need to remember why we started the journey, visualize the dream or goal we want to see made reality, seek out assistance and guidance, someone else to walk beside you on your journey. We need to find what kicks us back into action, into wanting to push further, so that we do not stall or stop altogether.

After all, it's great to get started, but it's not enough just to start. We must continue on, moving forward, conquering and prevailing until we reach our destination!

CONQUERING MOUNTAINS

There are always going to be mountains, some far taller or steeper or more treacherous than others. Sometimes we may climb them with others. But often, we climb them alone. And whilst the mountain can be a challenge in itself, it is not the mountain that we conquer. It is not the mountain that we face. It is ourselves. Ourselves that we fight against constantly; ourselves that is our real battle.

There is always some apprehension, maybe a little doubt or fear when beginning a journey we know nothing about, or that might seem "impossible", or when everyone else – and sometimes ourselves – are not even sure we can make it. But we can. We CAN make it if we just believe! We can climb any mountain, no matter how tall or steep or treacherous if we have the courage to take that first step onto the mountain path, the determination to keep going when it gets tough and the burning desire to reach the top, proving to ourselves and everyone else that we CAN do whatever it is that we put our mind to!

COMMITTED

EVERYthing you do counts for SOMEthing: A step forward or a step back; a smile or a frown; laughter or tears; progress or regression. EVERYthing you do should be to make you BETTER; constant desire to IMPROVE as an individual and in every facet of your life. For when YOU improve you unwittingly help OTHERS do the same.

What do you DREAM of? What do you THINK of? What ACTIONS are you making?

When you know what DRIVES you the DECISIONS you make become easy. For when you know what you want and are COMMITTED to it 120 percent you do everything you can to make sure it HAPPENS. You operate at 212 degrees with EVERYthing you do.

ARE YOU COMMITTED?!

NO EXCUSES

We ALL have 24 hours in a day. We all have a life filled with things like work, family, maybe study, some of us training, and even more of us other commitments. We all have the SAME amount of time each day in which to get things done. We are all going to do DIFFERENT things, based on our priorities.

That's the key word right there: PRIORITIES. If something is important to you, you WILL MAKE time for it. If it's not, then you won't, simple as that. Therefore, there are NO EXCUSES for why you did NOT do something if it is something that you really, truly want!

Make sure that you're NOT making excuses to why you "can't" do something and are always looking for a way to make sure it is an obstacle OVERCOME. When you stop thinking like a "loser", then you start winning in life; you start seeing things CHANGE. When you start taking accountability in and for your life, you become an EXAMPLE for others to follow. When others see the changes taking place in your life, it can inspire them to want to make changes in THEIR own lives, thus leading to a motivating circle of POSITIVE EMPOWERMENT, a ripple of effect more powerful than you could ever have imagined.

MAKE NO EXCUSES AND BE THE DIFFERENCE! IN YOUR OWN LIFE AND THE LIVES OF THOSE AROUND YOU! TODAY!

I CAN

It's all very well and good to have a dream, but a dream is just a dream unless you ACT on it, and a dream will not be acted on unless you believe that you CAN achieve it. Belief in yourself and your ability to achieve your dream is ESSENTIAL. You HAVE to believe that you can AND will accomplish what you want, or you will never really come close. If you believe, you'll take every challenge as it comes, won't allow difficulties to discourage you, knowing that you are one step closer every day to having what you desire, becoming who you want to be.

Your MIND is your most POWERFUL tool in the pursuit of your dreams. If you have no faith in yourself, no belief that you are capable, thinking that what you want is not possible for you, then you will never have it because you have already talked yourself OUT of it. But if you have confidence in yourself, believe that you can, and know that NOTHING is impossible for those who truly desire their dreams, then you are more than walking potential, and no matter how long the journey to get to your destination, you WILL arrive.

When you believe, you do everything you can to accomplish your goals, take the risks necessary, seek out the people who can help along the way, and do not allow the negativity of others to dissuade you from your path. When you have a dream and a vision you believe in, knowing that even if you do not have all the answers to everything that might happen along the way right now but just go ahead and start regardless, you will be able to overcome anything, something greater driving you through everything BECAUSE you BELIEVE.

It's not enough to want something. It's not enough to THINK that you can accomplish your goals. You have to BELIEVE in not just your dream, but in YOURSELF, and know that ANYthing is possible if you believe that "I CAN" do it!

IT STARTS WITH YOU

Desire.
Belief.
Motivation.
Inspiration.
Effort.
Progress.
Achievement.

LET NO ONE STOP YOU FROM PURSUING YOUR DREAMS!

How you live your life is ultimately up to you. Others may try and tell you what to do, and you may let them push you around, but in the end, the choice is yours and yours alone. There is always a choice. There are always consequences for every choice made, so listen to your instinct, that inner voice guiding you, and choose wisely! If it is in your heart to do something, then do it, and let no one stop you!

PUSH THE ENVELOPE

Life is not about playing it safe, staying inside four walls and never going outside of them, even for the smallest of seconds. Life is about living, experimenting, trying new things, opening up your mind and heart to the endless possibilities and wonder that lie in wait for each and every one of us.

Are there things we are apprehensive about? Absolutely. Do them anyway! Are there things that might frighten us a little? Sure there are. Don't be afraid; step forward with your shoulders straight. Are there times when we are taking risks that might lash back on us with consequences we have no way of foreseeing? Definitely. Take the risk anyway; you never know, it might be the best thing you ever did and one of the experiences you will never have wanted to miss out on in your life.

If you don't step out and try, you will never know. If you close yourself off to the limitless possibilities that life has to offer and holds waiting for you, then you are going to miss out on a lot of amazing opportunities. Don't let that happen!

PERSONAL ACCOUNTABILITY

There is always going to be someone with more talent, ability, success, or achievement than you. Just like there is always going to be someone who has less talent, ability, success, or achievement than you. No matter what, you are blessed just to have what you do and to have accomplished what you have.

Realize just how much you have been blessed. Appreciate where you have been. Take a firm grasp of the future, where you want to be and OWN your goals.

Make your word mean something. Make it mean something not just to others but to yourself; don't lie to yourself or allow your mind to formulate excuses for why you might not do what you know you must do. Instead, hold yourself accountable; know that the only person who you will really disappoint if you do not achieve your goals is you.

DEFINE YOURSELF

What are you? WHO are you? What DEFINES you?

Do you hold yourself to a higher purpose, your character so deeply imbued in all you do that no one can mistake what you stand for, your actions speaking of who you are? Or are you letting others dictate what you are doing with your life and who you are?

Don't let anyone else tell you what to do and who you are. Only YOU know who you are; anyone who thinks they do only THINK they do. So stand UP and be strong. Stand up and be YOU. Take back the power and make it clear that YOU DEFINE YOU! No one else has that right!

Define YOURSELF! Don't let anyone else do it for you (because believe me, they WILL try)!

It's YOUR decision! YOUR CHOICE! Your LIFE!

WITH PURPOSE

What drives you? What motivates you to do the things you do? What passion lies behind your actions? IS there a reason? Do you have a purpose?

If not, there SHOULD be! NOTHING you do should be withOUT purpose! Nothing you do should be simply BECAUSE. EVERYTHING you do should have a driving force, motivation, passion, PURPOSE behind it!

Life is a series of events and we have the ability to control some of them - not all, but some. The events that we DO have power over should NOT be random acts without direction but done WITH PURPOSE.

With purpose means to do with intent, to have an objective to achieve. What do YOU want to achieve? Think about it.

BRAVE ENOUGH TO VENTURE

Don't be afraid to make mistakes. Don't be afraid of setting off on a journey that you aren't completely sure of. Don't be afraid to go at it alone.

Some of the greatest successes in life come after making multiple mistakes, not knowing the complete process when began and finding out along the way, doing it alone because no one else has the faith to see what you see and believe in.

But to achieve those successes, you must first START. You MUST try. You must be determined to see it THROUGH, no matter the cost, time, or effort expended. There WILL be obstacles that you must overcome, sometimes more than moments of triumph as you applaud the next step up the ladder taken. Yet in the end it will be WORTH it.

Are you ready to IGNORE the excuses as to why you "cannot" or "should not" do what it is your heart desires to do? Are you willing to make a few mistakes on your path to success? Are you brave enough to venture out and become a PIONEER who will light the way for others to follow because you refused to give in to the thought that it could not be done?

Do YOU want to be GREAT?

SECOND CHANCE

None of us are immune to life and what it can bring, and we should always be prepared. Regardless, we should never waste a minute of the time that we have; stop procrastinating and start doing what we want to or have always planned on doing NOW. Start walking towards that dream, begin the journey that will take you where you have never gone before; step out in faith and know that everyone has that second chance, a chance to start over, wipe the slate clean and begin a new direction with their lives.

The world can - and will - try to break us. And we might break (it's okay) for a time. But then we stop. We realize. We understand. We KNOW. No matter what happens we can - and will - OVERCOME it. We will stand up. We will work THROUGH the pain. We WILL be strong again. We will show the world that while we are in it, we are not OF it. And THAT makes all the difference!

You might not see it now, but you will. Broken down to be rebuilt the way you need to, to become the person you were meant to be. Find your wings and fix what's been broken, so you can fly again. Transforming with every day that passes, growing stronger and ever more aware.

BE GOOD TO YOURSELF

Sometimes we spend so much time looking after and out for others that we forget to take care of OURSELVES. We work ourselves into the ground trying to do everything for everyone else, being strong for everyone else, making life work for everyone else, that we neglect to take care of ourselves. We allow our energy to be drained in service to others, our strength to be used to nurture others, our minds to be consumed by thoughts of how to make things better for everyone BUT ourselves. And when that happens, you have NOTHING left for yourself. You drain yourself dry. You don't nourish yourself, or replace what is being used, giving back to yourself so that you do not lose of yourself.

It's fine to give, but it's NOT fine to give and give and give until that's all you're doing, not taking care of yourself, not looking out for YOUR best interests, not accepting help from others because you have to be the one doing everything, until eventually you find yourself collapsing, shattered and broken, with nothing left to help yourself, empty and alone.

You have to be GOOD to YOURSELF. You have to nourish and feed yourself, whether it be taking time out every day just for YOU and no one else, meditating, filling yourself with the Spirit and refreshing your soul, speaking positive words of encouragement and empowerment over yourself and your life. You have to relax and recuperate, whether it is having a day off doing everything for everyone and focusing solely on you, so that both your body and mind stay strong without running out of energy or spirit. You have to learn to be selfish and say "no" sometimes because you cannot do and be everything to everyone all of the time, and you need to learn what you CAN do, what you cannot, and accept that, instead of piling all the world's burdens on your own shoulders.

You have to be GOOD to YOURSELF. When you are good to yourself, then you can be good to OTHERS. You are better equipped to deal with others and their demands, and you will not bleed yourself dry in trying to manage those demands.

You have to be GOOD to YOURSELF to be of any use to ANYONE ELSE! So, if you are not and know you must be, start today! BE GOOD TO YOURSELF!

YOU ARE CAPABLE

Sometimes we look at ourselves and we DOUBT. We doubt that we can do what we want, seeing only the obstacles and letting our fears get the best of us. We doubt that we can overcome the obstacles, blinded by the now and where we are now, forgetting that the now is not what will be or has to be. We doubt that we have what it takes, forgetting that God does not place a dream in our heart or on our soul if we do not have the strength and tools to achieve it.

We need to STOP doubting! We need to start BELIEVING!

Believe that you CAN do it; you CAN achieve that goal. See that dream become real, be who you want to be! Believe that you CAN overcome the obstacles; they are only there to see how much you REALLY want it, to make you stronger and better, so that when you are finally where you want to be, you are the BEST you possible. Believe that you DO have what it takes; everything you've ever wanted, dreamed, or had a passion for comes from someWHERE, and you wouldn't desire to achieve, see, be, or do those things if you didn't have what it took to get there.

All your doubts as to why you're not what you want to be, where you want to be, or doing the things you want to be are just EXCUSES. Get RID of those excuses and start BELIEVING IN YOURSELF, that YOU ARE CAPABLE and JUST DO IT!

I AM ONE

We are all only one part of life, one of many billions of people on the planet. The number one is a small, solitary number. It can be a common thought that "one" cannot achieve much, that it is INsignificant, but NOTHING is insignificant and ONE individual CAN make a difference, whether that difference is merely only to a single other or reaches out far beyond the scope of imagining.

There are many things that we cannot do simply because we ARE one. But there are also many things that we CAN do as one. Knowing the difference between them is a part of accomplishing great things; you must know when to "team up" and when you can go at it alone.

Even teaming up with another or a group of others, when the vision you share is mutual, for the greater good, IS making a difference. But the vision of ONE is nothing to be taken lightly either, for the vision of one can sometimes make the MOST difference; you just have to make sure that the difference is a POSITIVE and EMPOWERING one.

Therefore, NEVER UNDERestimate the power of who you are, what you say, and what you do. You never know who might be listening or watching and what impact you will have on them, on their LIVES, nor the subsequent impact that THEY can have on another.

Let your smile change the world and not the world change your smile, even if that change is for only one person and that person is you. All a matter of perspective, so choose to make it positive and live a positive life that inspires others to do the same and know that they too can keep going no matter what is going on around or to them. Choose your focus and you have chosen how you live.

PIONEER YOUR DESTINY

Not everyone has it in them to be a Leader. Not everyone can break away from the crowd and walk their own path, dance to their own tune, ignoring others' opinions on where they should be going in life. Not everyone has the courage to forge a completely new path through life – a path that OTHERS will follow.

PIONEERS are a different "breed". They are the dreamers, the innovators of the world, the visionaries. You might not agree with them, but you can't help but NOTICE them. They have VISION.

Even if they walk alone, they do not mind. They would rather carve their own path than simply blindly follow that of another. They set themselves apart from the rest, an inspiration to aspire to, motivating others to create MOVEMENT.

Every great achievement began with a VISION. And every vision was born in the heart of a PIONEER.

TAKE CHARGE OF YOUR DESTINY TODAY! BE A PIONEER AND INITIATE CHANGE!

HAVING VISION

Having vision means having a dream, yet not only having a dream, but seeing what needs to be done for it to eventuate, and being willing to do whatever is necessary to make it happen.

Many people have dreams, but not all of them have the courage to see past the obstacles they will have to manoeuvre in the pursuit of that dream. They fail to see what those obstacles MEAN, seeing them only as roadblocks and not as opportunities. They fail to see God in everything that comes to pass and walk as blind men seeking something they know in not what direction it lies.

Many people have dreams, but not all of them have the courage to turn that dream INTO a vision, moving it from their heart and soul into those of multitudes. Not all of them have the FAITH to stay strong to that dream through whatever may pass. Not all of them have the PERSEVERANCE to see it through to fruition and fall short of the glory that might have been theirs, of the difference they might have made.

Having vision means not only having your own dreams but seeing GOD'S hand in the midst of it. He would not give you a dream if He did not want you to DO something about it and was not going to be there with you every step of the way. God plants the seeds of vision inside our hearts for a PURPOSE. It's up to YOU to DISCOVER that purpose and then MAKE IT HAPPEN.

When you know your purpose, you truly know your heart. When you know your purpose, you are truly prepared to make manifest your dream. When you know your purpose, your vision is clear. When you know your purpose, you are READY to START CHANGING LIVES.

I SAY POSSIBLE

You say "impossible"; I say POSSIBLE. You say "can't"; I say TRY. You say "but"; I say DARE. You give excuses; I just ACT.

Life can be lived through INaction or ACTION. Everything has a consequence, whether acted on or not, the final outcome determined by the deed of the doer, whether they ignore what others said "could" be done and just go for it anyway, or stay immobile and eventually become stagnant in their journey because they refuse to venture out of their comfort zone and what they know.

Everything can SEEM "impossible" to those who have no vision, whose hearts and minds are not open to possibility, never willing to take the risk, but "impossible" is just a word, MEANINGLESS because ANYthing IS possible when you put your essence into a dream.

You stand by and watch; I get out there and DO. You're afraid to make mistakes; I see any made along the way as LESSONS. You don't want to get your hands dirty; I'm not afraid to be roughed up in the pursuit of my DREAMS.

At the end of the day will you look back and say, "I tried", knowing you gave it everything you had, or will you always wonder what "could have been"? That choice is entirely up to YOU. Your decisions and actions today determine where the journey of life will take you tomorrow, whether further or CLOSER to your dreams, only ever wishing for them or making your fantasy a REALITY.

ENVISION. BELIEVE. ACHIEVE.

Envision. Believe. Achieve.

For you to achieve anything, no matter how "impossible", "unrealistic" or "against the odds" it might be, you must first envision it, and then believe that you CAN achieve it. You have to see it clearly in your mind, as real as what you want to make it, an ALREADY tangible reality.

Every great accomplishment or dream begins with vision. You must know what it is that you want. You must know the path to follow to attain it and make it happen. You must know what you have to do, what you must overcome, and how you will overcome those obstacles, in order to bring it about.

Every great accomplishment or dream would not come to pass without belief. You must believe IN the vision, the dream. You must believe in YOURSELF and in your power to follow through with what must be done. You must believe in your STRENGTH to withstand and overcome any and all adversity that assaults you on your journey to making your dream a reality.

You have to ENVISION. You have to BELIEVE. Only then can you ACHIEVE.

DO NOT LACK CONVICTION

Do not lack conviction, least others doubt your sincerity. In everything you say and do, ensure truth and transparent consistency so that they do not doubt where your heart lies.

Conviction can rally others to your cause and garner support, entreat change to bring about a ripple effect more profound than you could ever imagine. Conviction stands you out from the crowd who do not know where their loyalty lies, who do not know their own heart and the desires hidden there, those looking for a leader who can unite them in a common cause. Conviction can move mountains, drive men to do the unthinkable, achieve the impossible because they believe in something greater than themselves, a higher purpose for the betterment of humanity.

Conviction is a powerful force, no matter how pure the motive behind it, so be careful what you hold so dear that you would be willing to do anything for and to protect, least you turn a multitude down a path that does not give to honorable cause.

In everything you say and do, have conviction and purity of heart. When such truth stands before men, it will change the world a little at a time.

IMAGINE. BELIEVE. ACHIEVE.

Your mind is your most POWERFUL ASSET. Never STOP IMAGINING. Imagine everything your life COULD BE. Imagine everything you WANT your life to be. Imagine all your dreams COMING TRUE. Imagine and ALWAYS GREATLY. Imagine that anything is ALWAYS POSSIBLE. Everything great ever achieved began in the MIND.

Belief is JUST as powerful as the mind. Belief lives in our HEART. It is part of the infrastructure that makes us what we are, WHO we are. It is part of the driving force behind our ACTIONS, determining whether we follow through with our imagining. Our hearts are not logical like the mind, and sometimes we will act on seemingly irrational things simply because we BELIEVE in it. Everything great ever achieved first had to be BELIEVED in.

If you IMAGINE AND BELIEVE, then you CAN ACHIEVE. If you want to achieve your imagining, then you must be prepared to WORK HARD, make SACRIFICES, GIVE EVERYTHING you have to your cause. You must be prepared to DIG DEEP within to find what you need, to accept what you find, sometimes things you might never have thought you had or were capable of. You must be prepared to face OBSTACLES, allowing them to make you STRONGER, not letting them deter you from your cause. Everything great ever achieved was not done without ALL YOU HAVE AND ARE.

NEVER let ANYONE hold you back from your dreams and ignore those who say your aspirations are too great. LISTEN to your SOUL; instinct knows and will never let go of anything you are destined to do or meant for in this life. CONNECT with LIKE-MINDED individuals who strive only to bring out and make the lights of others shine as brilliantly as their own on the path to the manifestation of their dreams. ENCOURAGE and SUPPORT the flames of change that flicker through your life and seek to be a blessing in every experience that opportunity grants. LIVE your TRUTH! FULFIL your POTENTIAL! BECOME your ULTIMATE!

WORTH IT

If you IMAGINE it and BELIEVE in your imagining, then you can ACHIEVE it. The path to achievement is not always going to be easy; more often than not, it is going to be one of the MOST DIFFICULT things you will ever face. But that doesn't make it something worth giving up on or letting go of; it makes it something to keep a firm hold of and KEEP STRIVING for. After all, anything worth doing is NEVER EASY; if you are patient and stay true to your chosen course, the FINAL RESULT will make everything you've been through to get there WORTH it.

Remember that whenever you are tempted to give up, for it is in those times, whether you give up or go on, that determines whether or not you reach the stars you are aiming for. And believe me, when you finally TOUCH those stars everything pales in comparison, your smile one you will never forget, knowing that every painstaking step of the journey to reach them was WORTH every sacrifice, every heartache, every tear, every sleepless night you spent to get there.

THE GREATNESS OF A MAN

"Greatness" can mean many things to different people. Not everyone is going to see it the same way as another and there will always be a difference of opinion. There are, however, two things that truly contribute to how "great" an individual is: Character and impact.

Everyone is flawed, but just because one is flawed does not mean that they are not of high character. A person's character is multi-faceted, but deep at the core of their soul is the root of their values. If that root is not founded on INTEGRITY, then one cannot truly be great, for everything they do is going to be based on something questionable, and when one's integrity is called into question, so is trust.

When trust is an issue, the impact is not always going to be positive and can cause more harm than good.

"Great" people are many things, but their very existence ALWAYS has a POSITIVE impact on other peoples' lives, intentional or not. A "great" person always strives to create an atmosphere of positivity, motivating others to have belief and faith in themselves, inspiring them to bigger and better things, so that their lives are as complete and as full as possible.

"Great" people are not always at the forefront of society, but they WILL be recognized within society for what they do, whether that recognition comes from a single individual or multitudes.

"Great" people do not necessarily set out to be great. They just are or become great because of the integrity of their character and the positive impact that they have on others' lives for the better.

OVERCOMING YOUR FEARS

Fear can be and instigate many things, inclusive of preventing one from stepping out and doing what they know they must in following their dreams. Fear is the small voice in your head telling you that you "can't" do it, whispering that you'll never be "good enough", the negativity that tries to make you think that no matter what you do it will never be of any significant worth. Fear is the killer of dreams, of passion, of opportunity. It holds you back, causes stagnation, prevents growth. It is an obstacle.

You need to OVERCOME fear. You need to overcome this obstacle in order to succeed in life. It is not going to be easy and many times you may feel like giving up, defeated and broken down from the stress fear gives your mind.

DON'T give up! Standing up to your fear and staring it in the face will make you STRONGER.

Strength comes from doing the things you never thought you could. It comes from going through pain and suffering, mental and physical abuse, standing up to and conquering that small voice in your head, refusing to back down or let anything keep you from moving forward for very long.

With strength comes wisdom. Knowledge of yourself and what you are capable of, how to draw from within yourself to find what you need, understanding the processes that allow you to overcome that which would see you "fail" in life.

There are times when a degree of "fear" is healthy, but many where it is nothing more than an obstacle to be conquered and overcome so that you can be become BETTER, and who doesn't want to be better than they are? Who doesn't want to be ALL that they can be?

BECOME YOUR BEST YOU!

PASSION AND DETERMINATION

Everything you do should be done with PASSION. Passion makes you feel ALIVE, lights you from within, gives the sparkle in your eyes, the bounce in your step, energy and enthusiasm that draws others to you.

Everything you do should be done with DETERMINATION. Determination means that you are prepared to do whatever it takes, no matter who or what may try and stop you from achieving what you have set out to accomplish.

Together, passion and determination make a POWERFUL team. A powerful team is hard to break and only gets STRONGER when faced with adversity.

Passion and determination make the journey less arduous. You know that everything done has a PURPOSE, bringing you one step CLOSER to the culmination of your dream. One step closer to the ultimate HIGH.

YOU DECIDE!

There are many people out there ready and willing to tell you that you can't do something, whether because they don't believe in your dream or you or just don't want to see you achieve something great. Don't let YOURSELF be one of those people.

At the end of the day, YOU decide what you can AND cannot do. If you believe in yourself and your ability to do something, then you WILL do it. If you do not believe in yourself or that what you want to accomplish is possible for you, then you will NOT do it.

The mind is POWERFUL. BELIEF is powerful. Self-talk can have a powerful EFFECT on the psyche, affecting actions and decisions, all which culminate to a destination. If that destination is NOT what you want to see or where you want to be, then ADJUST your THINKING so that your compass is set in the RIGHT direction.

After all, even if you tell yourself that you "can't", even if that small voice of doubt in your mind whispers it, you do NOT have to listen. You can CHOOSE to follow your HEART and forge AHEAD, impulsive or not, listening instead to your soul, acting on INSTINCT. THAT is how you get things done, how you achieve GREATNESS.

So go ahead. ABOLISH the word and thought "can't" from your existence. Reach for the STARS. Pursue the LOVE that consumes you. BELIEVE in YOURSELF. CHANGE your story. MAKE life work FOR you. YOU DECIDE!

THE SOUND OF A CHAMPION'S VOICE

Live to CREATE something. Live to make a DIFFERENCE. Live to CHANGE lives. Live to SHINE in the world.

Live NEVER giving up. Live ALWAYS trying. Live giving nothing but your BEST. Live with a PURPOSE.

Life is tough. It hurts. It causes pain. It will try to break you down.

DON'T give in. Pain is NOTHING. Defeat is NOT an option. You are STRONGER than that.

Life is for LIVING. Life is for moving FORWARD. Life is for experiencing as COMPLETELY as possible. Life is for standing up and KNOWING WHO YOU ARE.

You don't have to win medals or accolades on a grand stage to be a Champion. You don't have to have millions know your name to be a Champion. Being a Champion is in your ATTITUDE and what you DO. BE A CHAMPION!

THE STARTING POINT = DESIRE

Achievement is not accomplished from nothing. It starts somewhere. As an idea, a dream, a goal, a vision. It starts with a DESIRE. A spark that can just flicker faintly or turn into a raging fire.

Passion creates a burning heat that can't help but fan that spark into a flame. Passion fuels the flame and lifts the wind that breathes life into it. Passion stirs the life in that flame into a fire. Passion stokes the coals beneath that fire, to keep it burning bright. Passion lights the dark night with that fire as the flames rise higher and higher.

But if there is no wind, no passion, only a mere thought, a wish barely believed in, then that spark will never become a flame. It will only flicker, maybe flare briefly, but soon fade and die, disappearing into the wind as if it never existed, not even an echo of a shadow in the deepest dark of night, forgotten and discarded for all time.

Is your desire just a faint flicker or a fierce fire? If you want something, TRULY desire it, you will give nothing but your ALL to ensuring that it burns fierce and bright for the entire world to see, to spread so much light that you cannot see the shadows, drawing others into its circle. When your passion is such, it will not go UNnoticed, and the world will turn and watch as you pursue your dream.

When your desire is a raging fire, you will achieve GREATNESS because such vision cannot be hidden, only glowing brighter and brighter, until it garners support and encouragement from all directions, to see it fulfilled.

DREAM BIG. MAKE YOUR OWN LUCK. BELIEVE.

If you're not DREAMING, then you're not LIVING. NEVER be afraid to dream TOO big, for no dream is "too" big, not if it is precious to your heart and something you hold close. Dreaming gives you something to look FORWARD to, a PURPOSE to work towards, a HOPE to KEEP going, no matter what storms life throws in your path along the way. Dreaming is the first step to CREATING yourself, for as you dream and ACT on those dreams, so shall you BECOME.

"Luck" does not just HAPPEN. It is CREATED. It is created by YOU when you work HARD towards making your dreams a REALITY. It is created when you have something so STRONG in your heart that you canNOT let go. It is created when the heavens conspire WITH you to bring your dreams to FRUITION. Don't just "wait" for luck to happen. Make it YOURSELF.

BELIEVE in YOURSELF and in your DREAMS. Believe that your dreams, the hope in your heart, that it is all POSSIBLE. Believing is an IMPORTANT step to ACHIEVING. Without believing you have no MOTIVATION to act or create. You MUST believe. When you believe, you can become ANYTHING you want to be. Believe and CREATE yourself the way you WANT to. Believe in your POWER to ACHIEVE your DREAMS and watch as they UNFOLD before you when you step out and FOLLOW them.

GIVE UP, GIVE IN, OR GIVE IT ALL YOU'VE GOT

We all have ONE life. And we all have CHOICES to make. EVERY day. And it's those choices that will determine your QUALITY of life because Life IS going to kick you down at some point, and if it fails, it will try over and over. No matter what, remember that you ALWAYS have a CHOICE on how you RESPOND.

You can give up. Give up because it's too hard and all you see are obstacles, letting what you want go because deep down you're not sure you really want to achieve your goal, afraid perhaps of what will come if you DO. Give up because you listen to those small voices of fear and doubt that try and convince you that what you want is out of your reach, impossible for one such as you.

You can give in. Give in because you're not strong enough to stand on your own, compromising yourself easier than standing up and FIGHTING for yourself and your beliefs. Give in because you think that trying is not worth it, seeing only everything that could go wrong instead of everything that could go RIGHT, the endless POSSIBILITIES for change and GROWTH.

You can give it all you've got. Give it all you've got because you KNOW that YOU are in charge of your destiny, that if you want something you go out and GET it and MAKE it happen, refusing to believe that an obstacle can stop you from achieving what you want to, knowing that it is WORTH the struggles to get there. Give it all you've got because you desire with a PASSION to make a DIFFERENCE, wanting to EMPOWER others to have faith and belief in themselves so that they, too, NEVER give up or give in!

DO YOUR PART AND GOD WILL DO HIS

There's only so much that you can do in the pursuit of your goals and dreams. We cannot do everything alone, and even if we think that we are doing everything alone, we are never doing it all alone. Do as much as you can, all that is possible by yourself, and if you have to ask for help, then ask for help.

Asking for help is not weakness, but acknowledging that the achievement of a goal or dream is not an individual accomplishment; that it is a team effort, even if that team only consists of you and God. If you do your part as best as you possibly can, trust that He will do His part as well. God helps those who help themselves, and sometimes what happens is far beyond anything we ever imagined!

YOU ARE UNIQUE

We are all DIFFERENT. There is NO one person in the world exactly like another - past, present, or future. You are the ONLY you there will EVER be.

No one can do what YOU do. No one can love like you love. No one can give like you give. No one can spread joy like you spread joy. No one has the same talent and gifts as you do in the specific degree that you do. No one can REPLACE you and some things only YOU can do.

You are UNIQUE. EMBRACE your uniqueness. Do what you were CREATED to do.

LIVE LIFE LIKE

You only get ONE shot at life - unless you're one of the extremely rare individuals who have been blessed with a second chance - so make the MOST of it. DON'T waste it. REALIZE it and LIVE!

Never let anyone else tell you who you are and what you "should" be. Decide for YOURSELF and then BECOME it! Only YOU can ever be YOU. Only YOU have the unique "power" to make any difference that you do in the WAY that you do. Let your light SHINE and sparkle "through" life as you live in the world but not OF it!

Seek His heart. Listen to your soul. It will always lead you true. It is that little whisper of Him in your spirit that ultimately knows what's right for you. You'll feel the difference in your essence and see it in your smile. Even if no one else would ever understand.

Live while you have life. Take the risk. Follow your instinct and your heart. Fight for that precious to you. Give yourself permission to fly. Let His whispers in your soul guide you. You know where you want to be. Your tomorrow starts with today!

REASONS WHY I CAN

There are so many reasons out there why you "should not" do something, so many PEOPLE out there telling you that you "cannot" do something, but in the end they are merely that - reasons, and the opinion of others. If you should not do something take that into account sometimes, but the opinions of others telling you that you "can't" do something should NEVER factor into the equation on whether or not you do it.

People are always going to tell you that you "can't" do something, whether they don't want you to realize that you can do more than you thought you could, or don't want to see you achieve success above them, or some other reason. That is human nature; those who "cannot" will always try to convince those who WANT to that they don't stand a chance.

DON'T listen to those people. Don't let YOURSELF be one of those people!

We ALL have dreams; if you don't dream, what are you living for? When you stop dreaming, you simply exist, and simply existing is not LIVING! And we want to see those dreams become MORE than a dream. We want to see them become REALITY.

Instead of seeing reasons why you shouldn't or "can't" (because there truly is NOTHING that you can't do if you put your soul into it!), start seeing all the reasons why you CAN, why you SHOULD, and what happiness will abound in your spirit by following your heart and living out the journey of your dreams.

Go AFTER your dreams and watch what MIRACLES happen!

CHOICES, CHANCES, CHANGES

We all have choices. We all have chances. We all don't have to change.

We all have to decide to make a choice to take a chance if we want to change.

If you are not happy with where you currently are in life, then step back and reassess your situation. See where you are and where you WANT to be. Consider all the possibilities. Weigh in all the choices. Lay them all out before you and make a DECISION.

Your decision could be to stay where you are because your comfort zone is safer than risking the unknown. Your decision might be to take that chance and risk everything you know for what you don't, having faith and believing that putting yourself out there is the FIRST step to achieving your dreams.

Your decision to step OUTside your comfort zone is going to lead to CHANGE. Change is GOOD. Change means FORWARD momentum. It implies PROGRESS. Taking that first step into the unknown could forever change your life as you know it, but you will never know unless you TAKE it.

If you want your life to CHANGE, then you WILL make the CHOICE to CHANCE the roll of the life's dice and GO FOR IT!

DARE GREATLY, TO FLY

Whether I fall is not even in question. It's whether or not I put myself out there and take the RISK. Risk is one of the greatest things you can do in life. Sure, you might fall. But you also might succeed beyond your wildest imaginings. Besides, nothing great was ever achieved or accomplished by hiding your wings. It's time to take that leap of faith and trust that you can and WILL fly!

Anyone can do something they have no trepidation for. There is no courage in doing what takes no effort or risk. It is only when you do that which you are "scared" of that courage is shown and growth is made. Growth comes from OVERcoming your "fear" and taking that first step in faith as you risk (everything).

Some of us do what we do to show OTHERS that they too CAN do it. Just because we do something does not mean it is easy for us. We choose to lead by example to encourage and empower others into fulfilling their potential and living the most "complete" life possible!

FORWARD OR BACKWARD?

You have a decision to make every day of your life: Are you going to go forward or backward? Every decision you make, every crossroads, every turning point, will determine in which direction you ultimately go.

Those who know where they are going with confidence have faith in something greater than themselves, never hesitating to always do that which will always move them forward in life. Those who just wander aimlessly through life, or who allow themselves to never take risks because of fear, will forever stay stagnant or end up going backwards.

Do not let your fear rule you! Do not let it stop you from going out and taking the risk of chasing your dreams! Do not let it stop you from putting yourself out there and accepting the challenges that come!

Believe in something bigger than yourself! Believe that there are forces in this world far beyond your imagining that can make all your risks worthwhile! Believe that you have the power to overcome your fear and walk away stronger for it!

You must BELIEVE you can or you never will. Whatever you are striving for YOU have to see as YOUR REALITY before you will ever achieve it. If you believe in nothing else, believe in the dreams that persist in your SOUL.

THE PURPOSE OF LIFE

Life is for LIVING. Not surviving, but LIVING. And living is experiencing as much as possible, ALWAYS seeking to ENHANCE your life by trying new things, learning new things, growing INTO yourself as you become BETTER with each day. It's about EXPLORING your world with the eagerness of a child, OPEN to new possibilities, new experiences, CHANGE. It's embracing the new and letting go of the old when it is time to move on. It is keeping your heart and soul OPEN to receive the Blessings the universe has to offer and wants you to experience. It's about taking everything to the NEXT level, never satisfied with being satisfied, but always wanting to strive FURTHER, achieve more, evolving physically, mentally, psychologically, and emotionally into the person that you were always MEANT to be.

Not all comfort zones are beautiful places, but they ARE "easy", and one does not GROW when things are easy. One grows through challenges and struggle, when things are UNcomfortable. It's time to start getting "comfortable" with being UNcomfortable, taking risks and challenging yourself, enabling the best you and all that you have potential to be. Let your life be a living TESTIMONY and EXAMPLE of His Grace and Glory as you live by faith OUTSIDE any "comfort zone".

BELIEVE

Believe in yourself and the dreams in your heart. Believe in yourself and the goals you want to see manifest. Believe in yourself and the things you want to come true. Believe in yourself and stay true to yourself in everything you say and do.

Believe with all your heart that if it truly is important to you, NOTHING will stop you from attaining it. Nothing will stand in your way or say "no, you cannot do that", and if it does, you will knock it flying because you have so much faith that you are flying on the wings of hope, and hope is so very powerful.

Believe in yourself and what you truly want and know that ANYthing can be made possible, become possible, BE possible. Dare to dream OUTside the realm of what is "possible". Let nothing tell you that is it not, and if they do, do NOT accept it, for truth is what is and not one's opinion.

Believe in the heavens and the stars that light them and that you can REACH those heavens if you truly strive to touch the stars and be AMONG them. Do NOT limit yourself to what SEEMS possible or conventional and doable by man, but live by the dreams in your heart and ALWAYS BELIEVE.

REACH FOR THE STARS

NEVER think that what you want is too MUCH or OUT of your reach. NEVER let anyone else ever tell you that what you want is IMpossible. Ignore all the naysayers and those who are unsupportive of your dreams and goals; you'll often find that such people have NO ambition of their own and only want to bring others down to their level so that they can feel better about wasting their own lives.

CHAMPIONS REACH FOR THE STARS! They have a DREAM in their heart and they are NOT afraid to let it take root and CONSUME them, so EVERYthing they do is focused on that vision. Champions do not set the bar low; they aim as HIGH AS POSSIBLE because they have a deep desire to be the BEST that they can possibly be, and they do NOT accept anything LESS.

What is it that you truly want to achieve in your life? Do you think that you can "never" do it? If you do, then CAST those thoughts from your mind and seek out those who can - and will - help you on your journey towards the achievement of your desire!

DON'T accept anything less than what you know you are capable of, and once you reach that point push PAST it into the UNknown. I promise that you have so much MORE inside you than you realize, and that's what will make you a Champion!

Better BELIEVE it! Explore your POWER! Make a DIFFERENCE! BE the Example!

NEVER "settle"! ALWAYS strive higher and try harder! Give it ALL you've got and then go BEYOND your "limits"!

CHOICES & ABILITIES

We all have talents and abilities, whether we are born with them or develop them as we grow through life. However, not everyone USES the abilities they are born with, and some become adept at things that were not immediately natural to them.

Some would say that one is defined by what they can DO. Others would argue that it is not what one CAN do that defines who they are, but what they actually DO.

We experience many things in life, and two individuals who have gone through the exact same thing and grown up the "same" way will NOT turn out the same. Because we all have CHOICES; free will to decide what we will and won't do, whether we will be weak or strong, whether we will let our circumstances and experiences dictate what we are or whether we decide for ourselves who we become.

If we have a gift but never use it, can one say that that is what we are? We cannot, for it is our ACTIONS, not our potential, that defines us.

ACT ON YOUR FUTURE

One small step can turn into leaps and bounds and somersaults, and before you know it, you're jumping off cliffs into the open chasm below with arms wide open...

The first step is always the hardest. The first three weeks of getting up and going after something, trying to "reset" habits and patterns is always the most difficult. But you take that first step, get through those first three weeks, and everything after that becomes "easy", and before you know, when you look back you wonder why you didn't "start" SOONER.

STOP wondering. Start NOW. Don't be the one who looks back three weeks from now and KNOW where you could have been or SHOULD be and berate yourself for NOT doing it. Instead, SET your plan and know what you are going to be doing day-by-day to get you one more step CLOSER to your goals. Set your plan and then ACT on it.

Envision yourself jumping off that cliff and LOVING it. Imagine running through the waves on the beach and feeling the JOY seeping through every inch of your being. Reach out for the stars and know that you have it within you to be soaring through the heavens WITH them. Know that it is NOT a dream, but a reality just waiting to be "created".

And it's on YOU to create it. It's on YOU to be the change you want in your life. It's on YOU to take that first small step that will cause your "domino effect" of growth and achievement.

PUSHING PROGRESSION

Every day is a new day to not only make the most of what we have been given and to bless as many others as we can, but to push ourselves harder than ever before, in order to create the best physical body and spiritual being mentally, emotionally, and psychologically possible, for us each as individuals. For some of us this is second nature, but to most it is not. To the majority it is an effort, a learned approach to life, but not to say that it can't be embraced, accepted, and done, new habits created and formed.

It's a new day. If you don't see life as a CONSTANT PROGRESSION and TRANSORMATIONAL JOURNEY, then step OUT of the way of those who DO. Look at them as an example of what living life is about, of what you can do to start making a difference in your own life and the lives of those around you today. Make the decision: stagnation or progression.

Will you PUSH to become BETTER? Or are you content to stay as you are? Will you accept the challenge of changing the world what little bit you can? Or are you going to sit back and watch as others do it?

YOUR CHOICE!

STOP WITH EXCUSES

You ARE capable of achieving your goals. You HAVE the ability to succeed within you. You have the POWER to accomplish whatever you set your mind to. The only one holding you back is YOU.

STOP making excuses for yourself. STOP allowing yourself the "easy" way out. STOP saying "I can't do this because...". STOP blaming someone else for why you are not there yet. STOP shifting the accountability away from yourself.

If you have not yet accomplished your goal and you HAVE had the time, then you have no one to look at but YOU for it. No one else is responsible for it but YOU.

So STOP holding yourself back. STOP with excuses. Just get out there and DO it!

YOUR 100% TODAY

Your 100 percent today is not the same as it was yesterday, nor is it the same as what it will be tomorrow. That's okay. We change on a daily basis with what we are capable of, the intensity at which we are able to operate at, the effort that we can ask of our body. That does NOT mean that just because you cannot do what you did yesterday that you are NOT giving your 100 percent TODAY.

Life goes up and down and so do we. We have good days and bad days, days when we can take on the world and days where we only want to hide from the world, days where nothing can stop us and days when a single push could topple us over. We're only human and it's OKAY to be human.

As long as you enter each day with the attitude and determination to make that day as BEST you can and give your 100 percent, you will be okay. No matter what your 100 percent is on any given day, GIVE it, regardless of how you feel it is compared to times past or what you think it should be. As long as you give your 100 percent you are doing your best, and that is the mark of a CHAMPION.

YOUR 100%

Is your 100 percent REALLY your 100 percent? There will be days when your 100 percent is not going to be as much as it was on another. There will be days when your 100 percent will be far more energetic and enthusiastic. There will be days when your 100 percent will be absolutely amazing.

On the other hand, there will be days when you can barely drag yourself out of bed. There will be days when you are physically and mentally exhausted. There will be days when you do not want to be around other people. On those days, your 100 percent is going to be DIFFERENT to the days when you are a bubbly, bouncy personality who loves to be in a crowd.

It does NOT matter HOW you feel on any given day. As long as what you GIVE to that day in EFFORT in all that you do is your 100 percent on that day. Even on the days when you feel terrible, if you get up and you go to work, you smile and do the best you can with what you have in you, no one can ask for anything more. As long as you give your 100 percent on any given day, you have done what you can do.

RESULTS, NOT EXCUSES

There is ALWAYS an excuse that can be made. There is always a reason that could BECOME an excuse as to why something is not being done.

But excuses are NOT what I do. Excuses are NOT acceptable.

Excuses are made by people who canNOT take responsibility and have no accountability for what they do - not just with their personal life, but in every aspect of their life. Excuses are made by WEAK people, those who think that their failures rest upon someone else. They are made by those who want the world but are not prepared to DO what it takes to capture it. They are made by those who dream but never act, instead only trying to discourage others from pursuing their dreams because they do not have or are not willing to do what it TAKES to accomplish their own.

There is ALWAYS an excuse. You CHOOSE whether or not you ALLOW something to become an excuse. YOU decide what you do when life kicks you down or tries to destroy you. You create an excuse or IGNORE the naysayers and disbelievers and those who pretend to support you and secretly hope for your demise, and you get the job DONE. You GET results.

YOUR CHOICE. I DECIDE.

PUSH HARDER

YOU know what your goals and dreams are. You know what you have to DO to get there. You know what you ARE doing to get there.

You have to push YOURSELF. You have to push yourself HARDER. If you don't do it no one ELSE might, for everyone else has their OWN goals and dreams. If you want YOURS to happen, YOU have to be the one who makes it happen. YOU have to be the one in the arena fighting the battle. YOU have to be the one hanging onto the side of the mountain scaling it. YOU have to be the one jumping out of the airplane to skydive.

Ultimately your goals and dreams are on YOU. YOU are responsible for your progress towards them. YOU are accountable for what you do and do not do. You are the only one who TRULY knows how much your goals and dreams MEAN to you.

It's NOT enough to have goals. It's not enough to JUST dream. Nothing ever happened by simply DESIRING it. You have to PUSH yourself. You have to push yourself HARDER than ever before. You have to STOP settling for "okay" and start reaching for the STARS. You have to go PAST what you THINK you can and just get work done. Others may help with motivation, but YOU have to be the one propelling yourself FORWARD.

If you want to be the best, you have to strive HIGHER than you ever thought possible. You have to IGNORE those who say you "cannot". You have to see through tunnel vision your goals and dreams and stay FOCUSED. You have to push HARDER every day and leave nothing that should or could be done UNdone.

MAKE IT HAPPEN

What do you WANT out of life? Where do you see yourself in a year, five years, TEN years? What IMPACT do you want to have made? What do you want to be KNOWN for? The time to decide that is NOW. Decide and go AFTER it. CHASE your dreams. WORK hard to make them your reality.

If you don't know what you want, sit down and THINK about it. What do you have a PASSION for? What could you do for HOURS and it seems like time barely passes at all? What are you GOOD at? What SKILLS do you have? What are your DREAMS?

When you know, you HAVE to believe in yourself. You have to BELIEVE in yourself to be able to achieve. To achieve, you have to DO. To do, you have to start with DIRECTION. Your dreams, your goals, your ENDPOINT, give you direction in which to move.

You cannot rely on anyone but YOURSELF to make your dreams happen for you. It might take time, but NOTHING is impossible. Nothing is unattainable for the soul who wants it badly ENOUGH. You have to not just dream about it and go about it, but you have to believe it IS possible and WILL be your REALITY.

When you believe in yourself and your ability to make it HAPPEN, you pursue every course of action possible TO make it happen. You make life work FOR you. You SEEK the opportunities that will bring you one step closer to your dream. You ACT with your soul. You have to BELIEVE to achieve. Believe IN yourself. Make it HAPPEN.

THE DECISION TO TRY

Nothing great that was ever accomplished was done "suddenly". It did not "happen overnight". It was not a "random act". It was not a "coincidence".

EVERYTHING great that was ever accomplished was accomplished because someone had a VISION, a dream. They put ACTIONS to that vision, moved TOWARDS that dream. They decided to TRY.

You have a dream; I have a dream. We ALL have dreams. Not every dream will ever come true, because not everyone is WILLING to try. Not everyone is prepared to "take a chance", dare greatly and see what happens.

EVERY dream, no matter how "impossible" or "improbable" HAS the possibility of coming true. It might take time – days, weeks, months, years even. But it has the POTENTIAL. If it is a dream stamped with "greatness" or a dream that could inspire multitudes, its reality is INEVITABLE, but still, the FIRST step to "making it happen" is to make the decision to TRY.

NOTHING LESS

When you set a goal or see a dream, there should be NO doubt in your mind that you ARE going to ACHIEVE it. It might take you a week, a month, a year, longer, but there should be quiet confirmation in your heart that you WILL get there and see it become reality.

Nothing LESS is acceptable. When you desire something so much it consumes your soul and makes your heart burn and loops over and over in your mind, there is nothing but FOR you to make it HAPPEN.

Be a DOER, not just a dreamer. Be a PIONEER, not just one with great ideas. Let yourself SHINE, instead of hiding your light.

The world is crying out for those with the strength to say, "NOTHING LESS THAN THE BEST". It wants leaders who will BE the example. It wants those who hunger for "success" enough to inspire others to their own. It wants, so YOU be one of those people!

YOU CAN...MAKE IT HAPPEN

YOU are the one who ultimately determines whether you are "successful" or not. YOU have the dreams. Every day YOU make choices. The decisions are YOURS. YOU are the one accountable for the actions you take.

Don't JUST dream! Get out there and MAKE your dream come TRUE! Let it GUIDE you in your daily decisions. Let the passion for it FUEL your motivation. Make your motivation drive you BEYOND anything "comfortable".

"Successful" people LIVE their dreams day in and out. Even if they are not yet "real", they hold them so tightly in their soul, desire them like breath itself in their heart, and see them so vividly in their minds, that their BELIEF in their dreams MAKE them real before they are.

Dreams can drive you. But first you must make the CONSCIOUS decision to let them OUT and roar their INTENT. Remember, a dream is JUST a dream until you DO something about it. Intentions are NOTHING without ACTION.

You CAN do this! You can MAKE it happen! You just have to START!

GO CONFIDENTLY

Have CONFIDENCE in yourself and what you want to achieve. Believe that you CAN achieve it.

Confidence will take you places its lack will never be able to. It will open doors you might never have imagined. It will draw people to you in a way you never could without.

One with a dream is good. But one with a dream AND the confidence to put themselves out there for it is even better. And what makes that greater is the openness and willingness to RISK and SACRIFICE for that dream, for those who ACT on their dreams are those that can "change the world".

STAY TRUE TO YOU

Stay TRUE to yourself and all that you are. Hold tight to your dreams and goals, never letting anyone deter you from the possibility of them coming to life. Stay firm in your beliefs and convictions, steadfast in what you stand for. Never let the words of anyone who does not believe in you affect the decisions you make and the actions you take.

Hold your character in the highest regard, for it is the true measure of your worth. Stay strong and keep your heart for the one who will value it and see it as the most precious thing in the world. Never compromise yourself for fleeting moments of pleasure or the easy way out, knowing that staying true to yourself and working hard for what you want is the only real way to satisfaction of purpose.

Go after what you want with all the passion that you have, pouring yourself into everything that makes you happy and gives you a smile. Laugh at the world and life whether you agree with it or not, preparing to accept the good with the bad, the ugly with the beauty, the lies with the truth, because that is the nature of man.

Never let anyone tell you what to do and who to be, for they are not you and can never be, your life your own and no one else's. Take ownership of your life and stay TRUE to YOU – all that you are, can, and will be.

YOUR LIFE

Everything you do, everything you say, there is ALWAYS someone watching. Always someone taking heed of who you are, what you stand for, what you live for, your life message. What you have been through, what you have struggled with, what you have overcome, what you have triumphed with, is all a part of your life message, your life story, seen or told to the world.

We all suffer, we all fall, but we don't all push through the pain, we don't all rise. When you find the strength to survive and get back to your feet, it is INSPIRING to others, especially if they can relate to your struggle and pain, the circumstances, something similar. You can SPEAK to them without even saying a word, simply by your actions of strength, giving them faith that if you can overcome then they can too, that ANYone can, that it's POSSIBLE.

We all have success, but we don't all remain humble, and we don't always appreciate or acknowledge those who have helped us along the way, those who stand behind us, push us, believe in us and are always there. When you can have accolades too many to count, fame enough that multitudes know your name, but remain HUMBLE, striving only to use your success to HELP others, it speaks volumes of your CHARACTER and can say MORE than you might ever know.

When you are gone from this world what will be said of YOU?

BE THE CHANGE TO MAKE A DIFFERENCE!

If you want to change the world, you must first change YOURSELF. And once you have done that, you must surround yourself with those who are doing the same thing - changing themselves and living with a higher PURPOSE, those who want to CHANGE the world and make a DIFFERENCE. Seek them out and walk with them. Like-minds will also be drawn TO you, and together unite in your cause to make as much difference as you can, everywhere you can, to as many as you can, as long as you can.

Be a dreamer, a doer, a VISIONARY, a LEADER. Be someone who makes a DIFFERENCE, an IMPACT on ALL whose paths they cross and lives they touch, if even only for the briefest of moments. Be someone UNforgettable for the inspiration you light in hearts and souls, and bring your dream to MANIFESTATION. You were born for GREATNESS, and greatness makes a DIFFERENCE.

VISION AND REALITY

If you want something, you HAVE to do what you need to for it to HAPPEN. If you have a vision, you have to DO for it to become a REALITY. If you have a dream, YOU have to ACT for it to manifest.

Having a dream, a vision, wanting – it should all be about creating a BETTER you, someone who has a wealth of knowledge and experience behind them, unafraid to let the world see what they are because they are no longer that person. Your past may have created the circumstances that moulded you, but it does NOT define who and what you are; that is something YOU have to do for yourself, so stand STRONG and be CONFIDENT in knowing your vision, that the path you are walking is going to lead you to a higher place, a better you.

Know your PURPOSE and then SHARE it. Share it so that you can garner the SUPPORT you need to make it HAPPEN. You CAN do it on your own, but you never truly accomplish anything ALONE, even if it is a "solo" act.

Having a VISION means having a future that is not JUST for you, but makes a DIFFERENCE in the lives of others as well. YOU may be the one who gets down to the nitty-gritty because you know better than anyone what it is you want, but TOGETHER make it a reality.

RIGHT HERE AND NOW

Are you waiting for something to happen TO you? Are you waiting for your dreams to just FALL into your hands? Are you waiting for what you want to suddenly become a reality in your life? Are you waiting for tomorrow because you are too afraid of TODAY? Are you waiting without DOING, as if simply wanting is enough? Because it is NOT.

STOP waiting! Start DOING! What you want tomorrow has every possibility for being TODAY. If you LET it. If you let yourself HAVE it. If you BELIEVE in it and that you have every right to it.

You have every right to be HAPPY. You have every right to find PEACE. You have every right to SUCCEED with your goals. You have every right to be who you WANT to be. But it's all on YOU. You have to make it HAPPEN.

YOU have to be the one who starts the domino effect that will lead to the fruition of your dreams. YOU have to be the one to take the FIRST step into the unknown. YOU have to be the one to round up the resources that you will need on your journey. YOU have to be the one to hold the dream tight in your heart and believe with EVERY part of your being that what you desire the most IS for you.

Do that. Then watch. MIRACLES begin to unfold, dreams become your PRESENT.

I SHAPE ME

No one else can do it for you. Make you the person you want to be. It's entirely on YOU to do it. To take charge of your destiny and create it the way YOU want it to be. YOU SHAPE YOU. YOU have the power. YOU make the decisions. It's YOU. ALL YOU. If you don't like where you're at or what you're becoming, then CHANGE it. Don't wait for someone else to come along and make it better. FIX IT YOURSELF. DO IT YOURSELF. YOU have everything you need to become what you should be. Find it, use it, and BECOME. The onus is on YOU. YOU SHAPE YOU. Take CONTROL TODAY.

ONE STEP FORWARD

Each day is a NEW day. A new day to take another CHANCE. A new day to take ANOTHER step. Another step FORWARD in the direction of your dreams. Another step forward, no matter how small. For even the smallest of steps is PROGRESS towards the fulfilment of the ultimate achievement. The ultimate achievement of the ULTIMATE dream. Whatever that may be. For it is different to each and every individual.

No matter what, I canNOT be stopped. I cannot be stopped from TAKING that step. I cannot be stopped from reaching that one bit FURTHER. I cannot be stopped from STRIVING for "just one more". I cannot be stopped from doing my BEST, even if my "best" on any given day is not as good as it has been in the past or will be in the future. I will have given my best, my all on that day, and that is what MATTERS.

What matters is moving FORWARD. What matters is keeping the dream ALIVE. Keeping the dream alive in my HEART and the hearts of those I touch. For when I touch others, I make a DIFFERENCE. And when you make a difference, especially in a dream, you can CHANGE the world. ONE step at a time.

DO. CAN. WANT.

Being told you "can't" do something can be a highly motivating force. After all, who but YOU knows what you canNOT do? Not even you; you never know what you can do until you TRY. And if you "can't" do something and you WANT to, then you just KEEP ON TRYING until you CAN do it.

I do things because I CAN. Sometimes simply BECAUSE I can. Other times because I want to see what I can do, challenge myself, PUSH the limits, and see how far I can go.

If I do something, regardless of whether I "can" or not, I do it because I WANT to. Not because someone ELSE wants me to, but because I want to.

If it's something I want and I'm told "no", it just makes me MORE determined than ever to do it. Achieve it, not just because I want to, but to prove the disbelievers WRONG, to show the world that ANYthing is possible if you want it badly enough and are willing to do what it takes to do it.

DON'T ever think that you "can't" do something. Don't ever let anyone ELSE tell you that you "can't" do something. If YOU think you "can't", then you most likely never will (unless you use your own negativity as a driving factor, something only a rare few do and succeed with) because you will never try. If OTHERS think you "can't", IGNORE them and JUST DO IT ANYWAY!

COMPETITION OR NO COMPETITION

Some live life like a competitor - in-season and off-season, working hard in preparation for a competition, but letting go afterwards, allowing themselves to become lax in the excuse of the "off"-season. However, in life there is NO off-season; there is only the NOW. We live in the NOW. We live in the IN-season.

Whether you are preparing for a competition or not should NOT dictate how hard you work, how disciplined you are, how consistently you live. Competition or NO competition, your training ethic should NEVER change because EVERY day is a competition; you against yourself, and it is the HARDEST competition you will EVER face.

Live every day as if always IN-season. That's not to say that you can't allow yourself some time off or easier weeks; you should be doing this regardless because you DO need SOME rest, even when you think you cannot afford to.

Allow time to rest. Not just your body, your MIND needs that allowance as well, for it is the mind that drives us, and when we have weak minds, we are more likely to become complacent, and there is NO room in life for complacency.

Competition or no competition, life does NOT stop, does NOT get any easier - it is a perpetual battle for supremacy, a constant struggle to become BETTER than you were yesterday, a never-ending fight to become STRONGER, growing into the person you were always MEANT to be. And even if you get there, become who you were meant to be, it does NOT stop; there is ALWAYS room for IMPROVEMENT, and we should ALWAYS be striving for it.

THE WALL

A wall is nothing but an obstacle. And obstacles are always going to present whenever you are chasing your dreams. When one comes to a wall there are several types of people: Those who hit the wall and STOP, those who climb OVER the wall, those who see the wall coming and go AROUND it, and those who just keep going right THROUGH the wall.

Those who hit the wall and stop are a great majority. Sadly, these are those who will NEVER achieve anything great in their life because they are too afraid to take the risk or refuse to see the possibilities BEYOND the obstacles in their path. They are content to sit back and watch life, instead of being a PART of it. Ironically, these are also those who are the most likely to be the ones throwing stones and obstacles in the paths of those who ARE out there taking the risks and doing great things.

Those who climb over the wall are few. They REFUSE to believe that the wall is the end of their hopes and dreams, knowing that there is a way OVER every obstacle set before them. They are the thinkers, the doers, those who step out there and just do what it TAKES to get the task done. They are NOT afraid to fall, trying again and again if they do because what they want is far greater than the obstacles.

Those who see the wall coming and go around it are also few. They are the ones who are always thinking, always analyzing, always looking AHEAD. They are aware that NOTHING is easy, that there will always be obstacles, and they ALREADY have a plan before they come to any obstacles on how to deal with them, so that they expend as little effort as possible, being as EFFICIENT in the pursuit of their goals as they can be.

Those who keep going right through the wall are rare. They are the ones who refuse to let ANYthing stop them from achieving their goals and dreams, determined to have them at any cost, driven with a passion understood only by like-minded souls, possessing immense strength of both mind and body, believing and having such faith in their heart that NOTHING can stop them. They will do WHATEVER it takes and make every sacrifice to see their dreams made reality, even if it means that they come close to destruction in the process.

I know what I AM; what I DO. What type of person are YOU?

EVERY DAY IS A DECISION

Every day is an endless decision of opportunities waiting for us. Whether we make the "right" decision rests entirely on us, and we can blame no one but ourselves if we discard the path that would lead us to the success we desire. We can choose to step out and grab a hold of those opportunities, making the most of them, seeing where they lead. Or we can sit back, oblivious to them, waiting for something to happen TO us, instead of going out there and MAKING our own reality.

Life waits for NOBODY. If you let those opportunities pass you by, if you ignore them or are too blind to see them, then they WILL pass to someone else - someone who DOES want them and will make the most of them.

You have two choices in life. LIVE it. Or just be IN it. I know what I would rather do. What about you? Are you ready to go after your dreams today, to make the MOST of your life, so that you achieve and be everything you want and know you can be? If you know that you are, then GO OUT AND DO IT AND LET NOTHING HOLD YOU BACK!

ANYTHING YOU WANT

The world is YOUR oyster, YOUR playground, YOUR miracle. The place for you to make YOUR dreams a REALITY. But FIRST you have to BELIEVE.

BELIEVE that you CAN have what you want. BELIEVE that what you want is NOT "impossible". BELIEVE that you DO deserve the HAPPINESS your heart seeks. BELIEVE that you CAN do with your body what you see in your MIND. BELIEVE. BELIEVE. BELIEVE.

The MIND is your most POWERFUL tool and only YOU determine whether it will be a weapon TOWARDS the realization of your dreams or that which prevents you from ever stepping out and going after them. It's YOUR choice.

You truly CAN achieve the "impossible". I see MIRACLES every day. I LIVE a miracle every day. It's all on YOU what YOUR reality is because it can BECOME whatever you MAKE it.

"TOO FAR"

Life is not about playing it safe, living in a comfort zone. It is about taking risks, pushing the limits as much and as far as you can. For how can you ever know what it TRULY means to live if you limit yourself to living in a small square box, inside the lines that everyone else says you should stay within? You canNOT.

Those who dare greatly achieve greatly. They learn much about themselves and their strengths. They know what they are capable of and they are not afraid to push themselves further than before. They understand the risks but take them regardless. They realize that life is meant to be LIVED and experienced in its complete fullness, that there is far more out there than they could ever imagine, and that THEY are capable of far more than they might think or know in this moment.

Living life pushed to the limits, going "too far", does not mean being foolish in it, but simply accepts that you do NOT accept limits on yourself, desiring only to strive further, reach higher, achieve greatly, being a "miracle".

I live life on the edge, my body a living battleground. I've had a heart attack and yet refuse NOT to continue to push my body to exhaustion, training in all weather, on no sleep, when sick and knowing, looking at me, in no physical condition to be doing anything. I've collapsed multiple times during training, soldiered through the roughest times, determined not to let my physiological condition dictate what I can and cannot do, doing things others have told me I would never be able to do. I've suffered injuries and yet have come back from them stronger than ever and in less time than I was told it would take, taking a step further than the pain of returning to training, knowing that

if I do NOT ask it of my body, I will never have it. I ALWAYS push the limits because I would rather take the risk than NEVER know.
What about YOU? How do YOU live your life?

"EASY"

You say I make it look so easy, that it's easy for me, but how do you know what it's like for me? Stop judging and making assumptions based on what something APPEARS to be because what you see is not always the truth you THINK it is.

It might LOOK like it's easy for me to you, but what you DON'T see is the PAIN I feel with every movement, every second, choosing to IGNORE and work THROUGH it, instead of giving up because it hurts. What you don't know about are the YEARS of pain, the daily living in pain so much that it has become ACCEPTED as "normal", that "easy" is the furthest thing it is for me.

But you do NOT see that. How could you?

I'm not going to tell you I'm so tired I can barely keep my eyes open. I'm not going to tell you I'm so exhausted that it's taking all my energy and concentration just to stay standing. I'm not going to tell you the pain I'm in demonstrating something to you is enough to make me want to scream.

No, you just see me DO it and assume, creating an impression just as dangerous as an incorrect mindset. Unless you know, NEVER assume.

Live a day in my shoes and THEN tell me how "easy" it is. Live a day in my shoes and realize that I KNOW what it's like to feel and be weak and helpless, but that I choose NOT to let it determine what I can and cannot do. Live a day in my shoes and UNDERSTAND that I am who I am because I CHOOSE NOT to allow my struggles to control me, that I FIGHT back, that I BELIEVE I CAN AND SO I DO, and that in the end the DOING makes it WORTH it.

I do it because I want YOU to see that it CAN be done, that YOU can do it too, that you ARE stronger than you think, that you DO have it in you to SUCCEED if you WANT to, that the struggle is WORTH it. I do it because I care. I want to make a DIFFERENCE. I want to lead by EXAMPLE. I am who I am and this is what I DO. I FIGHT THROUGH THE TOUGH TIMES AND SO CAN YOU!

FITNESS IS WAR

We were born into a world where we must fight to survive, where war has become a LIFESTYLE. War against others. War against ourselves. There is no escaping it.

FITNESS is a lifestyle. It is a war. An endless battlefield of obstacles, of constant challenges and opposition. Day in and day out, strategy and planning, living to get through. Living to survive.

The enemy is not the ONLY thing you have to worry about. Your biggest threat is NOT the enemy. It is YOURSELF. It is not your enemy you fight against every day. It is yourself: Your fears, shortcomings, and weaknesses. Weakness can manifest in many different ways: Through excuses, indecisiveness, instability, and retreat. You must learn to overcome it, to conquer it, to set it aside, so that you can be victorious in battle.

There are times to sit back and observe, reconnoiter. This is NOT one of those times. This is the time to ATTACK. Be bold. Be strong. Hold yourself firm in your conviction. Surge forward, fighting. Hold nothing back. You cannot afford to. Once you commit, you COMMIT. There is NO going back, only going forward. Make each advance count, every sacrifice matter.

Live for this. Live to make your mark, to make your life count for something. If you live for nothing, you will die for nothing. That is no way to live, no way to be remembered. Be someone who moves from strength to strength and NEVER lets the word "impossible" hold any power. Be remembered for being a WARRIOR, a fighter, a survivor.

Fitness is a lifestyle. It is MY lifestyle. My war. Is it YOURS?

MY BODY. MY CANVAS.

My body is mine to sculpt. It is my canvas to create a masterpiece with; my raw materials with which to start off the rocky road to greatness. My body is my own and if I want it to be what I want, I must be the one to mould it, build it; create it. I must be the one who determines my limits and boundaries; if I choose to have any, to know how far I am willing to go, to push, to reach.

The motivation to create comes from within, the well deep down inside me, rushing from my core to the surface to design. It encompasses me so that I can think of nothing else but perfecting a masterpiece I am proud of, to show myself and the world just what I am made of. I, and only I, have the power to turn that inner source into something physical.

Every turn is mine to make. Every chip of the stone, every swirl on the canvas, is made by my hand and mine alone. I am accountable for the finished product; if there are flaws, then they are mine and I must accept that. I strive to do my utmost to work away anything that might detract from my masterpiece, to ensure it looks stunning from every angle, in any position, in every way possible.

I may stop and start many times over, but I always work on, each time better than the last, growing as I create, motivation building as I get closer and closer to what is envisioned in my mind. I am the artist. I am the sculptor. I am the designer. I am the one in control of who and what I become.

LIFE IS...CONTINUALLY BECOMING...

Life is about making yourself better. It's a continual process striving for perfection, even though perfection is impossible to attain. In the striving though, we can reach great heights, learn great things, and make a great difference. Life is about those heights, the learning, and that difference. We rarely get it right the first time; it's a continual process of experimentation to find what works best specifically for us, the best path to take to reach our destination, the best way to touch others so that we can help them with our knowledge and experience.

THE DIFFERENCE

Whether you believe it or not, there IS a difference between "giving up" and "starting over".

When you give up, you GIVE UP. You stop trying; you lose motivation; you refuse to see that you are closer to the end than you think; you allow negativity to control you and dictate your actions; you might never have had the passion and drive to begin with to see your goal through to the end.

Starting over is NOT giving up. It is realizing that some things are better UNdone than together, broken than complete; that not everything is meant to be or intended to happen, regardless of how much we might want it to be. Starting over is ACCEPTING that and giving yourself room to begin ANEW. It is giving yourself a second chance to get it right, to live your life the way it SHOULD be lived in order to be as complete and fulfilled as possible.

Others may see your "starting over" as "giving up". It simply means that THEY do not know the difference and have yet to learn the meaning. Give them time; not everyone learns life's lessons at the same rate, and some never want to know or acknowledge them. What matters is that YOU know it, and this is YOUR life, so LIVE it!

STARTING OVER

Starting from scratch can seem daunting. Sometimes it feels like the challenges might never end. Every corner you turn is something else. It can be overwhelming and you might need a moment now and then to gather yourself. When you do, remember...

Remember what it was like before and know that no matter how hard or how long it might take to rebuild, your eventual rebuild will far supersede anything you had. Because what you had you did not create. You did not start the building process. You had no input into the design. But now...

Now you hold the master sketchbook. Now you can start over. You can tear down anything that is detrimental to the overall purpose of your work. You can personally choose the components and help mould the moving parts that will be essential in your design. And when you are "done"...

When you are done you are never truly done. You continue building and improving. Continue remoulding, adding pieces, moving others around, a constant "work in progress" to always be "creating" something that works seamlessly together in the pursuit of a common purpose.

"WHAT IF?"

"What if?" makes you think about all the things that could have happened, that should have been different, if only something had not gone the way it had, if circumstances were changed, if life were "perfect". Unfortunately though, life is not perfect. In a theoretical world it might be, but we do not live in a theoretical world, and whilst there are theories abound in this one, even theories are not exact; even theories are not perfect. We live in a flawed world. Well, it is not the world itself that is flawed (God made it to be perfect); it is US that are flawed. And it is us that create the society we live in and the systems that govern that society, causing it all to be flawed.

Perfection is a dream. An illusion. However, whilst that may be the case, it cannot and does not stop us from trying to attain it. And that is the important thing; we must never stop striving to reach a state of "perfection", always pushing forward, always reaching up, always looking to become better than we currently are. That is what life is all about. Not what could have been, should have been, or might have been, but about what we can do NOW to make life different, more towards the way we want it to be.

PROGRESS IS A PROCESS

Progress does not happen overnight; it is a process that takes time. If you've just started exercising or changing your nutrition with the awareness of bettering your health and fitness, kudos to you. Just remember, if you look to your fitness role models for inspiration and motivation, that even they started somewhere, that their results are the outcome of years of "refinement" and striving to improve their fitness and physique.

Set your goals, but don't expect results now; don't expect results if you do not have the burning flame of desire, the determined light of commitment and discipline, and not without a lot of sweat and a few tears. Fitness is not a "magic pill", it is not a drink you take to get a "quick fix"; it is hard work and discipline. It is a lifestyle. As habits take time to form, so progress is a process, gradual, until one day you wake up and find yourself at the top of the mountain, ready to move onto the next slope.

Progress is never-ending, perpetually looking ahead at the next mountain, the journey sometimes easier, sometimes harder, but always a step up from the one you took before, you always better than you were before. Progress is a Process, much like the refinement of silver and gold.

BELIEVE IN YOURSELF!

Your mind is your only limitation, and, at the same time, the most powerful tool you have at your disposal. Success starts - and ends - in your mind. If you think you can't, you've already lost, but if you think you can, then you will most certainly succeed.

Belief is a powerful thing. Belief coupled with desire and action is even more powerful. After all, it all begins and ends with the mind. You must have faith and belief in yourself and your ability to accomplish your dreams!

Now go after your dreams, pursue life with a passion, and don't let anyone or anything stop you or tell you otherwise! No matter what, never give up, keep moving forwards, and always believe in yourself. You never know what you are truly capable of until you have to do it, but the strength to do what you have to in order to achieve your dreams is there, just waiting to be discovered (if it has not) or used.

TRAINING FOR YOU

Your training should be for YOU. It HAS to be. Otherwise, it will not last. You need to WANT it, the same way you have to want everything else that has a lasting presence in your life. It has to be about YOU, no one else. YOU sweating, crying, bleeding BECAUSE you want something to CHANGE in your life, READY to make the sacrifices, hurdle through the obstacles, do what you must to MAKE that change and have it PERMANENT. A permanent POSITIVE that will help you become BETTER, EVERY day for the rest of your life.

Once you start and you start for YOURSELF, no one else has the power to stop you unless you ALLOW them to, consciously or unconsciously making any decision that might take you away from the path you have set yourself upon. Once you have made the decision that what you are doing is for YOU, if you stop, it is NOT because of someone else, but because of YOU, and you alone are responsible. So be ACCOUNTABLE to yourself, know how much you want it, always remember WHY you started and what it MEANS for you to CONTINUE, and if you stop, realize that it is YOU who has stopped.

ALWAYS have a goal to focus on, motivation to keep you focused, inspiration to increase your motivation, and those who will be honest with you along the journey. After all, not everything can be self-driven, although when you train it NEEDS to be, but others can help push you when you will not push yourself because let's face it, sometimes we all have those days when we wonder what we are doing and forget that WE decided to do this, only needing that small reminder that it's all WORTH it to fight through the pain and FINISH what we started.

MAKE IT YOUR OWN

There is NO ONE else in existence that does what you do better than YOU, so OWN it! Make it your OWN! Put your personal SIGNATURE on it! Not just with your fitness, but in LIFE!

You are who you are for a REASON. You have a unique ability to turn the world into something wonderful just by being IN it. You are the smile in someone's life (least you forget it).

As far as fitness, NOTHING works the same for EVERYone. Everything affects each individual DIFFERENTLY. Therefore what you do should be for YOU, what WORKS for YOU, no matter what anyone else says or thinks about it.

LEARN as much as you can. EXPERIMENT with new things. Never stop seeking the next BEST thing, for your body NEVER stops CHANGING and YOU must change WITH it, ADAPT WITH it, CONSTANTLY be manipulating every factor possible to get the DESIRED result.

That's how you make PROGRESS. That's how you SUCCEED. Not just in fitness, but in LIFE! You make what you do your OWN because it IS your own. No one else can be YOU or do what YOU do.

FITNESS IS A LIFESTYLE

Your FITNESS is important, ESSENTIAL to overall soundness of body AND mind, to living a COMPLETE life. Therefore, it canNOT be something you only do "here and there", but something you do CONSISTENTLY. Fitness has to be a LIFESTYLE.

We all have ups and downs in our fitness, the way we do everything in life; that is normal. What is NOT normal is to use fitness the way you would fashion - as a trend, something you change based on how you feel or what is perceived as "normal".

Fitness should not be a TEMPORARY commitment, something done only at specific times of the year or when you want to achieve a certain goal. Fitness is an INVESTMENT - in your HEALTH and well-being, in your FUTURE. See the VALUE in that investment, in making that LONG-TERM COMMITMENT, even if you might not see all the benefits of it right now, because I guarantee later on, you WILL.

There will be times along the way when it will be hard and you might question the time and effort you invest in your fitness, but as with everything, it is to be expected; NOTHING worth doing ever comes easy or withOUT sacrifice. However, if you commit to your health and make fitness a LIFESTYLE instead of a "passing trend", you will NEVER regret it.

WHAT YOU ALREADY HAVE

Are you waiting for something to happen to you? For an opportunity to present itself to be able to put yourself out there. For someone to notice you and take the chance on you? If you are, prepare for disappointment because life rarely happens like that. Sure, there are a lucky few for whom everything seems to happen "just like that", but the reality is that such "success stories" are far and few between.

It's not about waiting for something to happen, or an opportunity to present itself, but about doing the most with what you have and the opportunities that you have already been given. Do that and those "new" opportunities will appear, more likely that you will be "noticed", and then you can make the best of those times to reach higher and strive further.

Are you merely interested or truly committed to what you want to achieve or are chasing? State your intentions and then act accordingly. Discipline yourself to ensure the most optimal outcome for that which insistently sits on your heart and soul. Create such powerful self-speak in your mind that there is no option available but the course you have determined towards your success. Live committed every waking moment and make your dreams reality.

100% CONSISTENCY

If you're not making the progress you want, or getting the results you desire, ask yourself if you're doing everything you possibly can to achieve them. Too many complain that they're not where they want to be, that nothing works for them, that they don't have the time, that no one understands. In truth, those are just excuses.

If you are following the right training programme and nutrition plan designed and created specifically for you for your goals and needs, there is no reason for you not to get results. If you are consistent in your training and nutrition and don't try to give everything a complete makeover or go from one thing to another every week, there is no reason for you not to make progress. If you really want something, you make the time for it, no matter how busy you are or what commitments you have. If you feel like no one understands, take some time to sit back and observe the lives of other people, especially those individuals who are successful at what they do and still manage to achieve outside of their family or work environments, and you'll notice that many of them face the same obstacles that you do, but instead of making excuses for why they cannot do something, they find a way to overcome their issues.

In the end, whether you succeed or not is just as much about what you don't do as it is about what you DO do. Think about it. If you're not prepared to do what it takes to get to where you want or achieve the goals you desire, then you cannot expect to make the progress towards them or get the results that you seek.

DISCIPLINE: Doing what you have to do even if you don't feel "up" to it!

If you want to SUCCEED, you must exercise discipline, risk, sacrifice, persistent in the pursuit of your dreams and goals. You will have to make choices and realize that there really is no choice if you are SERIOUS about that you chase. Even if you take a hit, stumble, or are knocked down, as long as you get back UP and determinedly keep fighting, eventually success and that victory WILL be YOURS!

IT TAKES TIME

Transformations do not happen overnight, nor do they happen just because you want them to. They take time, effort, discipline, commitment, consistency, and a burning desire to make them happen. You can want it, but if you don't take the necessary measures to do it, you will accomplish nothing. If you really want it, you will do what you have to, make the sacrifices that you must, and find a way to work through every obstacle placed in your path. It may take longer than you anticipated, or it might not. Either way, the end result, achieving what you set out to accomplish, makes it all worth it.

WORK IN PROGRESS

EVERY day is a day for self-improvement, betterment of not just mind and soul, but body as well. Every day we can build ON the one before, make progress, continuing FORWARD. Momentum NEVER stops, seeking only to keep moving, striding, running, leaping, as if there were no end and this journey endless.

You see where you are now. Look in the mirror and take note of the "rough sketch" you have to work from, the "base" that you have to mould with. Envision the CHANGES you want to make, seeing them as if they were real right now and know that they WILL be.

Tighten up the NUTRITION. Work WITH your body, not the self-sabotage you were doing before. NOURISH it. Remember that the "cleaner" your food, the better you will feel, for your body will function more smoothly on what it operates BEST on.

Drill your body through training like you were preparing for WAR. Treat it like a machine. Train it like an athlete. You want not just aesthetics, but FUNCTION as well, for there is little use in simply "looking pretty" when it comes to "real life".

Know your "limits", but do not let them stop you. Know them, so you know what to push PAST. Recovery is important, but timing is everything. Test yourself. In your mind, set NO boundaries, NO limits, so that you can surpass anything and everything you might ever have thought you could or would.

YOU are a "Work in Progress", a masterpiece being crafted in your own unique and special design. YOU are in control of how quickly you progress and where, so take ACCOUNTABILITY for your work. And because it is your OWN, let no one tell you what it should "be", but yourself. You are doing this for YOU.

JUST BE BETTER

It's not about being better than anyone ELSE. It's about being a better YOU. It's about being better than you were the DAY before, the HOUR before, the MINUTE before. It's about striving for CONSTANT IMPROVEMENT IN YOURSELF.

Everything done should have a PURPOSE. That purpose should provide a step not only towards your goals and dreams but in making you into the person you were MEANT to be. And the person you are meant to be is an ULTIMATE version of you; a constant journey of BECOMING BETTER.

It doesn't matter what anyone else is doing. It doesn't matter what anyone else looks like. It doesn't matter what anyone else thinks YOU should do and be. What matters is that YOU are following YOUR heart and working towards YOUR dreams, and your dreams are making you BETTER.

Use the time you have NOW. Not in the future, nor living in the past. Live in the NOW and create the BEST opportunities for you to evolve into a HIGHER being, throwing all limitations ASIDE and ignoring any negativity from those who seek not to support or encourage your personal and spiritual GROWTH.

Life is a journey. No, it's not JUST about you, but if you do not focus on you and becoming the BEST you that YOU can be, you cannot possibly give of your best and help anyone else become the best that THEY can be. Your life is an EXAMPLE to inspire and motivate OTHERS into becoming BETTER.

COMMITMENT, POSITIVITY, AND WILLINGNESS

Life is full of struggles, challenges that force us to rise to our POTENTIAL. Some see the hardship in the challenge and give up because they find it too difficult, whilst others CRAVE the challenge and seek every way possible to use the experience to BETTER themselves.

There IS a way through every challenge, if your eyes are OPEN to it, thinking OUTSIDE the box, nurturing creativity and GROWTH in your soul. There is an OPPORTUNITY to DISCOVER new aspects of life and to yourself, gifts waiting to be ACCEPTED and OPENED with wonder.

To FIND the way through life's challenges you have to be COMMITTED: To yourself, the goal, the dream, allowing your mind to filter away any negativity about the outcome, knowing that if you have faith it will all work out. Not always as you wanted or expected, but in a way that will only ENRICH your life, adding to the wealth of experience you ALREADY have, EXPANDING your mind and heart, and opening up your soul for even MORE blessings.

To get THROUGH life's challenges, you need to be WILLING to walk the path before you, no matter how daunting or unknown. You have to believe in yourself and your ability to OVERCOME, ensuring POSITIVITY even when your heart might feel faint at some point in the journey. Your willingness to WORK through the obstacles thrown in front of you reveals your soul, the way you seek to conquer them and see them as stepping stones to GROWTH.

Moving through life is a FORWARD journey. You cannot grow if you stay still or move backwards. You HAVE to move forward, ALWAYS forward, focused on the FUTURE stretched before you, knowing that you have LIMITLESS potential to create in it whatever you want it to BECOME.

COMMIT yourself to the path you have determined to walk. Be POSITIVE about your chances of success. Seek WILLINGLY the path less taken and carve your OWN. Stride FORWARD in FAITH and BELIEVE for the BEST.

BELIEVE

Believe in your soul that He only wants the BEST for you. Believe in your heart that dreams DO come true. Believe in your mind that you have only just BEGUN your journey to happiness. Believe with your eyes what a GIFT has been given you.

Believe and never stop believing that GOOD things DO happen. Miracles ARE real and they are EVERY day. He only wants to BLESS you with what you deserve. To TRANSFORM your soul so that you are ready to become the person you were intended to be. The person who will change the world where you are, little by little, piece by piece, touching the lives of those around you, to make what difference you CAN.

Believe in your soul that you are destined for GREATNESS. Believe in your heart that you CAN achieve anything you want. Believe in your mind that such joy as you desire is NOT out of reach. Believe with your eyes that the one standing before you is REAL.

Believe in the DREAM you find yourself walking in. Life CAN be a fairy tale if you open yourself up to the possibility. ANYthing is possible for the one who believes with everything they are, giving all they have, willing to step out one more time on the glass ledge and risk that they hold most precious. For NOT to risk is to potentially miss out on the greatest blessing that He ever intended for you to have.

Believe. ONE simple word. So much FAITH. BELIEVE and NEVER stop!

POSITIVITY

Every day starts with an ATTITUDE: YOURS. You choose how the tone of your day is set. Start it out with POSITIVITY. Breathe and open your heart with gratitude. A grateful heart is a thankful heart and a thankful heart sees the blessings before anything else, the possibilities in any challenge.

What you meditate on eventually becomes your reality. Gratitude and thankfulness give way to joy, a light in the soul that emanates out, casting an aura that affects the space you dwell in. You can change the atmosphere for better or worse; choose happiness and see how the world "changes".

HAVE FAITH

Worry takes away time. It ages your soul. It creates tears in your mind. It uses space that could be better occupied.

Worrying does not get you anywhere. Worry of what might happen. Worry of the future. Worry of whether or not you are following the right path. All these worries, and for what?

Worry destroys the time you have been blessed with by taking your heart's eyes off what is happening in the NOW, seeing instead of happiness everything that could possibly go wrong, envisioning the disaster that might occur, remembering the past and forgetting that this is NOT it. Worry takes us from the present into either the past or the future, one that is gone forever and the other not yet upon us, causing us to cease to live in the present. And the PRESENT is what is important, for we cannot change the past nor predict the future, but we CAN control what we are doing NOW.

Worry solves nothing. It does not do a soul good. It does not create harmony in one's heart and mind. It serves no purpose but to create problems where there are none.

A little trepidation about what is to come is natural, but we need not worry about (nor fear) it. Instead, have a little FAITH that you are right where you are SUPPOSED to be at this point in your life, surrounded by the people you are MEANT to be surrounded with, loved by the one your life has been leading you TOWARDS, writing a future that holds nothing but GREATNESS.

Faith gives HOPE to a soul. It supersedes all worry and fear, giving you calm inside your essence that everything will turn out all right, knowing that God would NOT have brought you to this place if He had not intended you to learn or become something from it, if He knew you could not handle it.

Faith is a POWERFUL tool, a weapon against the worry that seeks to destroy. It allows you to see the light in the darkness, be able to take that first step out into the unknown, trust that your soul knows what it's doing, and that your instinct will not lead you wrong. LET yourself have faith and TRUST in it. Trust in yourself and in Him, and know that the world is a wonderful place where ANYthing is possible and dreams DO come true.

RISK TO SUCCEED

Life is made on gambles and nothing is achieved without first taking a risk. Progress is not made without change, and closing one door opens up new opportunities and possibilities. No one ever got anywhere playing it safe.

If you want something, the onus is on you to make it happen. And it WILL happen if that's what's in God's plans for you, but you can't leave everything up to Him; He gives us our desires, passions, and dreams for a reason, and it's not to sit on them!

You do what you have to when you have to, and when things change, you adapt to ensure constant progress. Life is always moving and we move with it, running with the ball we are thrown. As long as you learn along the way, appreciate the beauty in life and see the experience for what it was, you'll be fine.

Keep moving forward. Always forward! Big things come from big dreams and having the courage to risk pursuing those dreams! Sometimes we have to things we don't want to do in order to achieve the things we desire. LIVE life and don't just make it an experience!

TAKE CARE OF YOU

If you do not take care of YOURSELF, you will be in no shape to take care of anyone ELSE. To be able to give your BEST to the world, it's time to take care of YOU.

No more letting yourself go, even though you have been HAPPY the last few weeks. No more "I can get away with it" because it has been shown that you actually cannot any longer if you are not TRAINING. No more time off from training, even if your body HAS needed it. No more allowing yourself to sleep in, even though your body has welcomed the REST. No more comfort, even if you have enjoyed it for the FIRST time in your life. You may have been happy and enjoyed it, and it may have helped you in SOME way, but it has NOT been conducive to your health and well-being. It has NOT been kind to you and is NOT "taking care" of yourself.

NO MORE letting yourself go! No more COMPLACENCY! No more "It'll be okay when I get back on track" attitude. It's "back on track" NOW and NO going BACK! No more backwards motion! Only FORWARD!

You were doing just fine before. You were in a good place, comfortable physically, and you WILL be again. You were finally SATISFIED with where you were and now it is all gone, but you CAN AND WILL be in that state again. Only this time you will be BETTER! AND you will be HAPPY, able to allow yourself to ENJOY life and MAINTAIN that satisfaction (in your body) withOUT any complacency, striding only FORWARD with your life because the future holds so much for you!

DON'T SETTLE

There comes a time in your life when you say, "Enough is enough", "This is not me", "I will not let myself live like this anymore". Your soul, heart, mind, and body have great "memory" of the discipline you "lived" in the past – one part of the past that was truly an asset, and an asset that once had, never truly lost because the ability and "habit" is already ingrained in who you are, and no matter if it seems "lost" for a time, is always there to be found and used again. The "memory" of the lifestyle "before", the "good", that which allowed progression and growth – that is all there, slumbering awakening, a dull rumbling beneath your skin, like the groaning of a volcano ready to erupt. LET it out; let it loose to be YOU again.

Settling was NEVER an option; "comfort" may have been slipped into, but once realized, can no longer be allowed. Motivation for everything you want and need is there; it has just been hard to "move". But now there can be no excuses NOT to; there is no one but you to whom you shall eventually be accountable for what you did and didn't do in the pursuit of your dreams and desires. Those who achieve great things did not settle; they may have been "knocked down" or out for a time, but they did not let that stop them, and on the rise back up, found "new" strength and growth that serve them in their surge forward. Forward momentum – habits might be hard to break and make, but once made, can be made again, better than before.

Chase your dreams with a vengeance; don't let anything stop you, any obstacles serve only as "lessons", milestones of growth and progression, keeping your mind objective as your heart focuses on your vision and purpose. Go after what you want; you KNOW you are worthy of it, accepting of yourself and what has brought you to who and where you are now, even as you know that you cannot and will not "stay" where you are now. You are all about becoming better on every level, being the example for yourself that you are YOUR competition, leading by example that no matter what one has faced or is facing or will face, they CAN always OVERCOME and CONQUER!

SUPERSEDING HEIGHTS

Once you reach one height, achieve one goal, manifest one dream, it's NOT the end. Your journey is FAR from over.

Life is all about BUILDING on what we have accomplished, becoming BETTER every day, EVOLVING perpetually until we are the BEST that we can possibly be, the ULTIMATE version of ourselves, what we were always MEANT to be. It is a NEVER-ENDING process because we will never completely be the "ultimate" version, but we CAN achieve satisfaction in a life well lived, fully and COMPLETELY.

Once you reach one height, set your sights on an even HIGHER peak, a greater goal, a new dream. Then APPLY all the DESIRE and DEDICATION that you have within you to REACHING it.

And when you reach it, REPEAT the process and KEEP repeating it, for life is about constantly moving FORWARD. That is how GREATNESS BECOMES.

NO SHORTCUTS

Life is TOUGH. It HURTS. It lets you achieve the pinnacle of "success" and then it kicks you down a cliffside faster than you can think. That's life. Get used to it.

Get used to it. But DON'T accept it. DON'T let it beat you so much that you give up trying altogether. Don't let it take away the ESSENCE of you and the spark that keeps you going and burning bright for others to see.

Life is tough BECAUSE it is PREPARING you for what is to COME. It has to make sure that the you that eventually reaches the destination intended is a you that can LIVE there. It has to make sure that you have what it TAKES to live the life you want and achieve the dreams in your heart. It has to make sure that you're STRONG enough to look fear in the face and release courage despite any and all odds.

The journey may be long AND hard. But without the journey the destination would not hold as much MEANING. It would not be APPRECIATED for the sacrifices required and the work that it took to get there. It would not see a soul that had been tested by fire and trialed through destruction come out as a "brand new" being capable of the ultimate AWARENESS of self and its world. It would not see a soul who understands that the true desires and dreams of the heart are worth EVERYTHING endured to get there.

Shortcuts create DEFECTS. Life wants to make sure that there are no defects in the "end creation" that steps into its final place of realized PERFECTION. It wants to make sure that the soul that holds its dreams in the palm of its hand is one who KNOWS the explicit emotion of having experienced the world through more than a looking glass. It wants that soul to see the DUALITY in everything and understand just what it takes to stand on top of the world and look out over it. It wants a soul who knows its darkness and light and CHOOSES to live its truth in light.

STOP looking at only what one LOOKS like or what they DO. START looking at WHO they are, what they've been THROUGH, their MOTIVATIONS; then you'll REALLY start to "see" the truth. Just because one looks a certain way or makes something look "easy" doesn't mean they always have or it is. Some of us only "look" as we do or make it look "easy" BECAUSE of YEARS of discipline, pain, and sacrifice, and just because we did it then doesn't mean we're still not doing it NOW. Hard work is CONSISTENT. SUCCESS is PERSISTENTLY AND CONSISTENTLY WORKING HARD, but also having the ability to EXPERIMENTALLY ADAPT TO AND WITH CHANGE, driven by DETERMINED MOTIVATION AND DEDICATED PASSION towards a PURPOSE!!!

FIGHT FOR YOUR SOUL LIFE

The first step is deciding what you want. The second is knowing what you have to do to get it. The third step is the hardest but the one that starts the journey and that is ACTION.

You have to BELIEVE so hard your conviction creates daily inspiration to keep pushing FORWARD. Reset your mind so that there are NO excuses and only the "impossible" dreams and limitless potential waiting to be achieved.

And if you're going to fight, you have to give it EVERYTHING; otherwise, you're not really fighting at all. But first, you must believe in YOURSELF; that you can overcome anything thrown at you. You have to WANT it, and know WHY you want it; simply wanting something without reason is wasting life that could be spent in pursuit of purpose.

It's all about INTENSITY. The harder the battle, the more worthy that which is fought for. The tougher the struggle, the more precious the soul that comes out "the other side". A strong mind controlling a strong body can overcome ANYthing. It's not about what it looks like, but how it WORKS; if it looks good but doesn't function or is "rotten" inside, it's useless.

FOCUSED DETERMINATION

That way you get in the gym when nothing and no one else exists but you and the weights, feeling the pain and incredible high making it almost pleasurable, being so "in the zone", your "happy place", a sanctuary from the rest of the world's realities – consider living EVERYthing in your life with that same focused determination. If you already have or do, you'll understand how it can make everything seem more meaningful, hold purpose, and give you a reason for "continuing".

Life may not be a "training zone" per se, even as it is, for as you live you are being "trained" in the ways of life – conditioned, moulded, taught, created, evolving; a living entity constantly changing, affected by the stirrings of its soul and the emotions wrought within it by its experiences of the world and those it touches as it passes by. Imagine seeing every experience and person as a "lesson" or a "reason" to help you learn or understand your "mission" and develop deeper meaning for the purpose you discover your soul living for.

Focus your soul on your purpose. Let it seep into your heart. Allow it to become all that your mind dwells on. Create your lifestyle around it. Act out the directives that will ultimately bring you one step closer to your "destination", even as each new destination reached only means that the next location on the journey is revealed because the journey of life is one that is never-ending.

Focus with such determination that you cannot see anything outside of your purpose. Know what you will and will not allow in your life. Become a master at inviting the growth you need and weeding out the inevitable toxicity that will seek to undermine and destroy you on your path to "success". Listen to your instinct and be not afraid to walk away from anything that does not make your soul sing or gives you a creepy feeling.

Let yourself "become" your purpose, so much that anyone who looks at you sees the focused determination and inexplicably knows that you are a soul on a mission. Like souls, hearts, and minds will be drawn by your determination, the unwavering facing of whatever comes, perhaps seeking to join or walk alongside you as you brave and carve the path you choose to take.

Whether you are aware of it or not, that focused determination will inevitably ultimately inspire others, either to "find" their own purpose or to join you for however long it takes to "become" the conviction and strength that you exude for themselves. Sometimes we are what others "need" to get set on their own path, even as others may have been for us a turning point in "resetting" our lives.

FOCUSED DETERMINATION. It can create so much. It can become so much. It can change so much. Find YOURS. You never know WHAT it could do!

THIS IS YOUR LIFE

It's a mindset. A vision. A way of living. Be so focused on your vision that you instinctively move away from anyone or anything who is not moving in the same direction. FORWARD. Choosing growth and empowerment. New experiences and an enriched life.

Every day is a new day. A fresh start. A blank slate. You choose what you draw on the easel of that day. Make it a work of art that people REMEMBER. That they will want to stop and look at. That speaks to something deeper within them than simple surface logic.

It's all a choice. And it's all on YOU. How you decide will ultimately determine one step closer or one step further from your vision. Each day is an opportunity of possibility. Each moment to be lived with nothing less than passion and soul.

LIVE "GREAT"

We should never start the day withOUT thoughts of greatness. We are not born to be "average" or "fit in". We are born unique and different, destined to create footsteps where there are none.

Mediocre should be a word stricken from thought, NEVER to be considered or contemplated. We are living masterpieces and masterpieces are never "mediocre".

When you wake up, thank Him for another chance to do something GREAT, see your dreams in your mind, feel them in your heart, and envision what your "chance" can be used to accomplish.

Make a DIFFERENCE. Leave a mark. Live with PURPOSE.

SHAPE YOUR FUTURE

TODAY is where you stand. Today is what you have NOW.

What do you want your future to LOOK like? What do you want it to HOLD? What do you want it to BE?

Decide now. Determine the necessary steps. Take ACTION. Remember what you do TODAY sets the course for your FUTURE.

Focus your mind on your dreams, goals, hopes, aspirations. Give attention to what is important. What you dwell on will ultimately become your reality, so make sure it's what you WANT.

It's up to YOU to shape your future. Here. Now. Today. START.

YOUR MIND

Your most powerful weapon and best tool. The most dangerous control or greatest gift. And you choose what it will be. You decide. YOU.

You ultimately determine whether or not you control your mind or allow it to control you. Decide NOT to let it "just happen". Consciously take charge.

Reinforce your "reactions" by being IN control. You are an emotional being capable of extreme logic. Create a balance to achieve your best action.

Through it all, never lose sight of your soul. Your vision. Your purpose. You can both control AND be free. It is not easy. But it IS possible. BE.

HUSTLE

Some might say, "Good things come to those who wait" or "If it's meant to be, it will be". That's all very well and good, but I believe that if you want something, TRULY want it, you'll go AFTER it and work for it, doing whatever it takes to make it your reality. Waiting on "fate" is inaction and yes, while there are times for patience and "seeing", life does NOT wait, and often YOU have to go out and MAKE it happen. YOU. YOU have to decide whether the decision of your action or lack thereof will be worth the risk and you can live with "What if?" or you truly want NO regrets in life BECAUSE you DID your part to work to make it happen, no matter how hard it was or despite any doubt or fear you may have had.

START. USE. DO.

Start NOW. There is no better time than NOW. There is no EARLIER time than NOW right now to START the road to your dreams. So if there is something you want to do, then set the wheels in motion for it to be accomplished NOW.

Use what you HAVE. It is INSIDE you. It can be found AROUND you. You will find that you have what you NEED when you start LOOKING and are ready for it. When you start on the journey to a dream, others JOIN you.

You can do no more than your BEST. Your "best" changes every moment, so every moment you must be aware of yourself. Be aware of your feelings, thoughts, and emotions because ALL of it affects your ability to "perform".

Start NOW. Use EVERYTHING at your disposal. Do ALL you can do and then SOME.

ALWAYS A WAY

No matter what anything LOOKS like, there is ALWAYS a way for those who are determined and can look BEYOND what is seen. Circumstances may seem "impossible", challenges and obstacles insurmountable, but for those who refuse to believe that nothing is as it seems, ANYthing can be "resolved".

Learning to see past the visible is a stepping stone to growth and understanding. It reveals a different kind of soul: One who is not afraid to take risks and try new things, who revels in challenges and unlocking "secrets". It OPENS a soul to a "new" world full of possibility and "magic".

There IS always a way for the dreamers, for those who dream in the light become the PIONEERS and the leaders of this world, "symbols" of "success", even if at first they were mocked and disbelieved. Let your SOUL guide you and "show" you everything possible in the "impossible".

RELEASE

Sometimes we need to have discussions with others because they may ask questions we do not consider, view aspects we do not realize as "important", seeing us and the world through "fresh" eyes and a change in perspective. I had a conversation a few days ago that caused reflection; a question asked that made me sit back and think because I had never considered it before. Why is it that we can "not" do certain things when they seem so simple? What is "preventing" us from doing it? What is "blocking" the "flow" of action and ease of interaction with not just others but also with ourselves?

What IS it that is holding you BACK (no matter the area of your life)? You might need to search deep to find the answers; it might be uncomfortable and difficult and there could be inner turmoil as you struggle with your demons in the darkness and depths that have to be ventured into, but when you find those answers life will become much EASIER. You need to be OPEN to what you find, understanding that the answers may not be what you thought; perhaps an issue you never even realized was an issue or something long thought resolved. Whatever it is, you need to "see" and KNOW it with your ESSENCE.

To do that you have to uncover whatever it is that is holding you back, do more than "discover" it because that is just the first step of the process; you need to not just "see" it but UNDERSTAND it and truly KNOW in and with everything that you are because only when you do that can you ultimately RELEASE it. When you release and "let go" of it you can then "speak" far MORE than words. When you speak "knowledge" from your CORE and not just from your mind, you are one step

CLOSER to being able to walk and live the life you want (and need).

You OWE it to yourself to take that step; to stop and reflect and ask yourself the "hard" questions you might not have wanted to ask or not known until now to ask; to search BELOW the surface of what "appears" to be to what truly IS; to understand and get to know yourself on a level you might have never known before. When you are in true alignment with your soul you need not doubt, but simply act; everything else becomes simpler; life becomes simpler because you know what you need to do and have NO hesitation or unconscious inhibitions in doing it.

INVEST IN YOU

THINK about your future: Where do you want to be? Think about the cost: What do you need to sacrifice to get there? Don't think about the opinions of others on your decision; you have to do what will be best for you!

Think about your future; your life is yours to live. Think about the cost; realize the expense of NOT daring greatly in pursuing your true heart's dream. Don't think about trying to figure everything out from the beginning; sometimes the simple decision to just start is the catalyst for everything else.

Think and DO. Invest in YOU.

YOU ARE ALLOWED

STOP limiting yourself. What you can. What you won't. What you don't. It ALL matters. Your THOUGHTS matter. Your actions MATTER. EVERYthing creates SOMEthing. Don't be what's holding you BACK. Be what lets you surge FORWARD. Be the arrow. Be the flame. Be the CHANGE. LEAD your own revolution. Do it for YOU. Become your BEST self.

Aspire. Perspire. Inspire.

New day. New start. New chapter. Let yourself turn the page and move forward into the future waiting. The first step is always the hardest but it's the most important. New time. New beginnings. New YOU.

LOVE YOURSELF

To embrace your skin and be comfortable in it, you truly do need to love yourself. To be happy and move forward with life, you need to love yourself. You need not just to accept who you are, but love yourself too. Everything ultimately goes hand-in-hand if you want to achieve your complete potential and be the best version of you possible and create the life you really want.

Loving oneself is one of the hardest things in the world. While self-acceptance can be easy, it is not interchangeable with self-LOVE and has not the same effect. Yet you should not wait until you are happy with who you are and where you want to be in life to love yourself. Start NOW. Sounds so simple, but often the simplest things are the hardest to do. But do it and discover that the smallest shift in mindset can be all the difference and create the biggest change in your life.

DARE GREATLY

Whether we want to believe it or not, it all comes back to us. The onus for our life lies on ourselves. And the overall state of it really does come down to how we feel and think about and treat ourselves. Yes, sometimes, even when we know better, we let external forces influence and affect how we feel and think and act. It's called being human and I am as flawed as any.

Yet making mistakes does not mean that we are not imperfectly perfect and cannot be happy right here and now. So I choose to forgive myself for my "mistakes" and see them as lessons in my soul's growth. I already accept and embrace myself as I am, and while it is an ongoing process, some days more of an effort than others, I choose (again) to approve of and love myself regardless of anything and everything.

It is time to take a step back and rediscover what it means and be the love for myself that I have been for others. It is essential to follow and do what makes my soul happy, for ultimately it will only aid in serving energy that inspires and helps awaken awareness, change, and growth in others.

RISK AND CHANGE FOR GROWTH

Change is intended to create and cultivate GROWTH, using circumstances which force you to reevaluate your life so that you can see and let go of whatever might hold you back. Often, whether we are consciously aware of it or not, or want to admit it to ourselves, FEAR is one of those things: Fear of becoming even more vulnerable or letting it be known, of leaving a "comfort zone" because it may be the only thing familiar to us, even if we are very uncomfortable there and want a "way out", but being honest with ourselves that we have no idea of what to do or where to go next.

Growth IS uncomfortable and can make you vulnerable because it is often made in the most intense situations which place us in a position where NOT reaching out to another may cause further devastation, but it is a huge step because trust can be so thin because of experiences preceding the "turning point" of honesty with yourself about what is happening. It takes a lot of courage to confide in another soul, especially when your history has almost always been alone or loyalty betrayed, but sometimes people DO surprise you and you may find more than just a glimmer of hope if you risk taking that uncertain step.

Risk can sometimes be the test of whether or not we are truly ready to move FORWARD, for without it, taking that step, making a decision that we have absolutely no idea where it will take us, there may never be real opportunity for growth. Sometimes we HAVE to take that first step of trust to begin to "see our way again", blurry as it may be, because it means we want to move forward no matter the cost, knowing that anything is better than merely existing like we have felt became a way for a while.

Even if you have almost always "traveled" alone, there are times when it is better for your own well-being, and essential for your increasing enlightenment, to welcome the company of another soul beside your own. And not just for you, but for that soul too, it may mean the first step in their journey of courage and risk, desiring to break free from all that keeps them immobilized, willing to let go of any and all fear, to begin the process of truly LIVING again.

> "TAKE A MOMENT...GIVE THANKS FOR HOW FAR YOU'VE COME, HOW MUCH YOU'VE TRANSFORMED AND HOW MUCH YOU'RE STILL...DAILY"

I am not the only one who has dealt with and is still dealing with things throughout and in life, and while no one's struggles are the same, the emotions and feelings experienced may be similar. Those struggles are by no means any more or less significant to that individual than another's are to them, especially as everyone is different and not everyone is built or equipped to handle things the same. I want to remind you that whatever has happened in the past is BEHIND you and that while it may have helped shape you, your true power is in the PRESENT moment; not then or in the future but right here, right now.

It might not seem like it, but right NOW you have the power to choose - what you want, what you will do, how you will respond (if you respond), and when you will step into or further towards everything that will become the future. Every day we change, even if it might not feel like it, whether it be something that seems so small as a thought, that you later realize as a big shift in mindset. Every day. Small things add up. Every step you take. Every change you make. Everything is part of the ongoing and enlightening transformation to your highest awakened evolution of self.

All those struggling right now, I want you to look back, but only for a moment, and only to remember where you were. Now see where you are; realize how far you have come from there, how much you have overcome, how much you have changed to be able to do that, how much of a victory it is to still be here, and be PROUD of yourself - your heart for keeping you going even when it might have wanted otherwise, your mind for persevering, yourself for every victory no matter how small, and your growth through it all.

    Being here, today, alive, is no small thing, and it should be appreciated. Now stop looking back and look FORWARD. Being alive means nothing if you are not LIVING. So give yourself permission to LIVE, today and every day that you are blessed to have, and make every moment count as much as possible.

God never gives us more than He knows we can handle, and everything we go through is for a reason! Obstacles are there to test us; to see what we're made of; what we're capable of, by how we respond to them; to build, improve and mould our character, refining us; to make us more ready to fulfill our purpose in the world. They reveal how much we really want something, what we're willing to sacrifice to achieve our goals and dreams. They should inspire determination and motivation to overcome, no matter what! So, stop making excuses today; have faith and look at any and all obstacles as a challenge, readying yourself to conquer them and grow!

GIVE IT YOUR ALL

No matter what you are doing, whether it is a small task or one of ginormous proportions, always do your best. Always give it everything you have, the very best that you can in that moment. Even if you don't feel like it, make an effort. My mother once commented that I "could be dying and no one would ever know because you'd still be doing everything". An extreme example, yes, but illustrates that you can use every opportunity to make what you are doing mean something, whether you feel like it or not. Make everything you do count for something, no matter if you think it significant or not, because you never know just how much difference it can or will make in someone else's life.

Just another day, but not just another day. Another chance: To be, to dream, to live, to love, to learn, to grow; to see the blessings and wonder that hide in a simple smile or a look; to know your life has purpose and value, that you are precious to more than you might realize; to discover that your world can be created or destroyed by what you let creep into your heart, changing your perception through thoughts that ultimately become actions. Embrace that chance, challenge your heart, and seek to experience all He intended for you; to become all you were meant to; to make all the difference that only you can.

BE REAL

No one is perfect. We all have flaws, no matter how hard we might try to hide them or pretend that we have none. Man is not without sin, and so we are all imperfect beings. And that's okay. It's okay to be imperfect; it's okay to be flawed. And it's okay to let others know about those flaws.

It is not the strong person who always appears to have everything in control, who never missteps, who has the "perfect" life, that people relate to. It is the humble one not afraid to let the world know when they struggle, who allows others into their world to share those experiences, and who then uses those experiences to help others deal with similar situations.

It's through our struggles - most often brought on by our flaws or as a result of them - that we relate to others, that allow us to have compassion and understanding of another, that bring us together and create bonds of friendship and fellowship.

BE AWESOME

Even the best of us make mistakes, have "down" days, and need our time alone. That's okay. It's HUMAN. When YOU are in such a place, remind yourself of this. Remind yourself that you were created to be a MASTERPIECE. Masterpieces are beautiful and mean or show something different to all who perceive it. The one thing they are not is "perfect", which is what makes them MORE beautiful. Remember that. You are perfectly imperfect and your uniqueness is AWESOME.

KEEP TRYING

So you "failed". You got let down. You were disappointed. That's life. It happens. The world is full of imperfect people. Including you. That's not reason to beat yourself up over it. It's in the past now. So let it go. See the lesson. Learn it. Move ON.

KEEP TRYING. You might "fail" again. But you also might succeed. And that is why you take the risk. Because if you never try you can never succeed. If you never try you can never fail. And if you never fail you will never learn. Without learning you will not move forward.

HOLD ON. Sometimes hope is the only thing that keeps us here. Even when we feel like giving up. Sometimes all we need is that one thing to keep us going. That one dream. That one hope. That one spark that burns no matter how dim or bright in our soul.

ALWAYS BELIEVE. You might be the only one. But you won't always be. Not when the world "sees" you. Not when they see you make things happen. Despite all the odds stacked against you. When they see that something higher drives you. When they see that you will always keep on going.

CHIN UP. You're a fighter. You're a warrior. You won't let them "win". You won't give them the satisfaction. More importantly it's not about them. It's about you. What you are made of. What you have within you. What truth lies in your soul. The only thing you have to prove is to yourself.

KEEP SMILING. Life goes on. Whether we stand or fall it does not matter. But every time we fall we need to get back up. We need to look up at the stars and see ourselves there. We need to reach within and find the strength to try again. We need to remember the good we have and keep it close.

So you "failed". There is still beauty in the world. There is still hope. You're not the only one out there who has. But you can decide whether or not you will be one of those who allow themselves to be defeated or one of those who refuses to accept defeat. Because there is still chance to get it RIGHT.

BE YOURSELF!

There is only one you in the world. Only one being with the unique make-up that you have. One in the entire existence of everything. Have you ever wondered why that is? Why there never has been and never will be anyone else exactly like you? It's because God made you like that. He designed and created you to be unique. To be special. He created all of us thus. So that we would all work together and contribute to the whole, and in doing so, live the lives we were meant to lead. Therefore, don't bother trying to be like someone else or something that you are not. Instead, embrace who and what you are and be the best you that you can possibly be!

> "WE WILL NEVER BE DONE BECOMING... LEARNING... DREAMING..."
> —ROSIE CHEE

PHOTO BY TONY MITCHELL

CAN'T IGNORE YOU

Accept who you ARE. Embrace what you are BECOMING. ALWAYS strive to reach the stars. Do your BEST in everything.

When you do what you love, you do it with determined passion and enthusiasm, and it SHOWS. You GLOW, and when your light glows, you draw others to you.

You CAN be good at something you have no passion for, but that will also show in time - if it does not to begin with - so be sure to put your effort where it will bring not just joy to others, but to YOU.

Hone your skills to PERFECTION. Become an EXPERT. When you do what you love with a passion and you EXCEL at it, people can't HELP but notice. When others notice, the world can start to OPEN up for you, new POSSIBILITIES you might never have imagined before spread before you. And when that happens, you can affect MORE people, make more DIFFERENCE, create more CHANGE, and bless MORE; a true gift indeed.

YOUR LIFE IS YOURS

You have to be the one who is happy with how you live your life. You have to be happy with what you have done, are doing, and will continue to do.

If you're not happy, then do something about it. Don't feel like you have to live your life in a limited and tiny box to please everyone else, or you'll just end up hurting yourself and likely feeling resentful. If you want to do something, never mind what anyone else thinks. If it is your heart's desire, do it!

There are many things in life that others will not support you with or approve of, but it's not their life to live, so live it doing what gives you the greatest satisfaction, to achieve your definition of "success". Sometimes the things that are the most worthwhile and give the most accomplishment are those you go at alone, dancing to your own tune, with your own vision and dreams.

If others cannot accept your choices and decisions, that's on them, not you. Live knowing that you are doing what you love, making the most difference that you can.

YOUR WORK

When you stop paying attention to what everyone else is doing and focus on what YOU are doing, the world becomes a much simpler place. It also means that as you do what YOU must do, you need to trust that everyone else is doing THEIR part.

When you focus on what you need to be doing instead of devoting your energies everywhere else, you can create something much BETTER because your concentration is completely on YOUR task. You can ensure that what YOU do is done as well as it possibly can.

When you fill your role to the best of your ability others NOTICE, drawn to the passion emanating from you, something that they might not be able to explain, but which could change them in ways no one could ever predict. Your actions, though silent, speak as loud, if not LOUDER, than any words you might say, and sometimes those actions are exactly the words that another NEEDS to "hear".

When your work draws others to you and makes an IMPACT on them, that impact spreads, like ripples in a pond, no matter how small the ripple or how small the pond. You make a DIFFERENCE, whether you know it or not, and you want that difference to be a POSITIVE one, so stay focused on YOUR purpose and just let everything else happen as it will and does.

YOUR HERO

You are a HERO. Yes, YOU. When life throws you down, even if you stay there for a time, you are NOT defeated and it is NOT the end. Sometimes you need to fall in order to find that which has been hidden or lain dormant. And when you do, rise UP and fight BACK.

Be your OWN hero and refuse to let the odds dictate the strength in your fight, the passion in your eyes, or the courage in your heart. If you want something, YOU go out there and MAKE it happen, covered in blood and sand in the gladiator's arena, as life seeks to destroy you. Refuse to be destroyed and only come back BETTER and STRONGER every time you get knocked down!

YOU DECIDE!

There are many people out there ready and willing to tell you that you can't do something, whether because they don't believe in your dream or you or just don't want to see you achieve something great. Don't let YOURSELF be one of those people.

At the end of the day, YOU decide what you can AND cannot do. If you believe in yourself and your ability to do something, then you WILL do it. If you do not believe in yourself or that what you want to accomplish is possible for you, then you will NOT do it.

The mind is POWERFUL. BELIEF is powerful. Self-talk can have a powerful EFFECT on the psyche, affecting actions and decisions, all which culminate to a destination. If that destination is NOT what you want to see or where you want to be, then ADJUST your THINKING so that your compass is set in the RIGHT direction.

After all, even if you tell yourself that you "can't", even if that small voice of doubt in your mind whispers it, you do NOT have to listen. You can CHOOSE to follow your HEART and forge AHEAD, impulsive or not, listening instead to your SOUL, acting on INSTINCT. THAT is how you get things done, how you achieve GREATNESS.

So go ahead. ABOLISH the word and thought "can't" from your existence. Reach for the STARS. Pursue the LOVE that consumes you. BELIEVE in YOURSELF. CHANGE your story. MAKE life work FOR you. YOU DECIDE!

START STRONG. END STRONGER.

YOU have a goal. You have a DREAM. You WANT to ACHIEVE it with ALL that you are. It is IMPORTANT. It MEANS something. It SAYS something about you.

You STARTED with a PASSION. You went HARD out of the gate. You covered the PLAINS, went OVER the mountains, found your way OUT of the trenches, and now you can see the END in SIGHT. Your pace has wavered as you journeyed, slowed since you started. But...

You are going to dig DEEP and pull EVERYTHING you have. You are going to do WHATEVER it takes. You are going to PUSH yourself until you can push no more. You are going to strive HARDER than ever. You STARTED strong. But...

You are going to end STRONGER. You are going to cross the "finish line" and have NOTHING left. You are going to be able to say you truly gave it ALL you had and held NOTHING back.

I CAN. I WILL.

Act on your own words.
Take your own advice.
Live on your terms.
No excuses no regrets.
Your life is your own.
Take ownership of it.
Do what makes you happy.
Live on your own terms.
Now and every day.
Live to the full while you can.

Chase your dreams and kick away your "fears". Take every risk your soul encourages and ignore that which would hold you back. Let go of anything and anyone who cannot "see" you and be thankful for the ones who know and accept you as you are. Step away from the past and into the future. Open your soul and heart and mind to the blessings awaiting you. Walk into the dawn with new hope and renewed faith. Embrace what is coming.

Make a difference. BE the difference. Set an example. Be THE example. Encourage and persevere. Conquer and achieve. For His Glory. Always.

I AM MY MOTIVATION

Motivation has to come from within or it won't last. Knowing where you've been and where you want to go helps fuel resolution to keep going, even when it might make sense to no one but yourself. Every day is one more step in the journey. It's you versus you, becoming better than you were no matter what happens along the way. Find your spark and make a promise to yourself to always see it even when you cannot feel it.

---

x Photographer: Walt Ostarly.

Sometimes those who are the most "motivational" are simply trying to motivate themselves; to remind themselves to keep leading by example; that sometimes true living is not just surviving, but existing in such a way to be the something they would want to aspire to be inspired by; to prove that anything is possible. Sometimes those who try to make everyone else smile and strive to help others, the one always there for everyone it seems but themselves, are the ones who are struggling the most but who stay "okay" no matter what, laughing as they cry, smiling through the pain because they know that energy is contagious and regardless of anything going on in their own lives, they only want to infuse positivity into the lives of others. Sometimes those who seem the strongest have been the weakest when rare few others have seen or know of it, and it is that weakness, the fall from grace and hitting absolute bottom so that knees are left bruised and bleeding amongst the shattered shards of what they used to live and be, that transforms them into a weapon of both destruction before recreation, transformation and healing, enabling them to do as they do and smile to the world, be positive and motivate, knowing life is about something more than they, with a higher purpose that has a role only they can or might ever be able to fulfill. Sometimes what impressions are or what seems or appears to be is the furthest from the reality of what has been or is; everyone has a story and everything a reason; we're all here to help enlighten and enable each other to become the best we possibly can, so let no one forget that.

UNFINISHED WORK IN PROGRESS

We are all an UNfinished "work in progress", simply because we will NEVER be done BECOMING. We will NEVER be done LEARNING. We will NEVER be done making mistakes and finding out how to FIX them. We will NEVER stop DREAMING and STRIVING to REACH those dreams. We will NEVER stop SEEKING to do ALL we can to make as much DIFFERENCE we can. We will NEVER allow ourselves to just STOP and give up when life gets tough. We will NEVER allow ourselves to crumble in the midst of ADVERSITY. We know our struggles will only create in us something STRONGER and more POWERFUL than we might ever have thought possible.

We will ALWAYS be working TOWARDS something NEW, something GREAT, something that will leave a LEGACY of HOPE and FAITH and BELIEF. We will ALWAYS be working THROUGH the pain and fear and heartache and loss that we deal with in life, to LEAD by EXAMPLE that life kicks ALL of us and we do NOT have to give it the power to destroy what we are BUILDING.

We KNOW we are CAPABLE of far MORE than we have done and can ever fathom. We know that in order to BECOME all that we are MEANT to be, we must LIVE life and EMBRACE it with all its smiles and CHALLENGES, because it's the JOURNEY that is going to REVEAL the TRUTH and MAKE us into what we WILL be.

LIVING STORIES

There is a story in everything. A story about life. A story about transformative healing. A story about the time your world first collapsed around you. A story about how you survived it. A story about why you are still here even after.

This world, the people, the nature, the soundscapes, all have stories, and if you look or listen hard enough, seeking from your own heart's soul eyes, you will see and find.

So many stories. So many lives. So much repressed before revelation. So many slowly being brought back into the light of the darkness they found escape to.

There is a story in EVERYthing. There is ALWAYS a story. You just have to find it, begin it, to understand how they came to be as they are now, so that through true empath capabilities, you see every side of every side, every ugly in the dark of light hide.

The world is full of stories. Stories are all around you. The potential for desired probably reality is gargantuan.

Being a role model means leading by example. Everything I am and do is a testament to what can be done if you but have the faith in something bigger than yourself and allow yourself to be used to fulfill your purpose, always having the belief that anything is possible. I hope that through everything, I can provide something for others to draw motivation and inspiration from.

ℜ Photographer: Tony Mitchell.

ABOUT THE AUTHOR

Rosie is a Kiwi*, who has more recently made herself a home Stateside.

She has taken on many roles in many lifetimes. Each, however, has the same mission statement (albeit altered) and core essence (freesoul truth), and that is TO HELP PEOPLE. Whether that is by helping them find and understand their purpose, inspiring or motivating them for change in their lives (lifetimes past she was more notably known for her roles in the health, fitness, wellness, and supplement industries as an athlete, exercise physiologist, representative, and writer for companies, magazines - inclusive of online global giant Bodybuilding.com - amongst other things), or simply just BEING, her heart and soul are to MAKE A DIFFERENCE, no matter how small, whether she knows or not.

"CONNECT WITH THE ESSENCE OF YOUR SOUL"

---

* A Kiwi is what someone from New Zealand is called.